D0913031

DIVISION OF LABOUR, TECHNICAL CHANGE AND ECONOMIC GROWTH

To Tito, whose love gives me strength

Division of Labour, Technical Change and Economic Growth

MARCELLA CORSI

Avebury

Aldershot · Brookfield USA · Hong Kong · Singapore · Sydney

3 3 8. 9
C 8 2 d

© M.Corsi, 1991

Published by
Avebury
The Academic Publishing Group
Gower House
Croft Road
Aldershot
Hants GU11 3HR
England

Gower Publishing Company
Old Post Road
Brookfield
Vermont 05036
USA

A CIP catalogue record for this book
is available from the British Library.

ISBN 1 85628 231 7

Printed in Great Britain by Athenaeum Press Ltd, Newcastle upon Tyne.

Contents

List of figures   vii

List of tables   ix

1   Introduction   1

I   THE CLASSICAL CONCEPTUALIZATION OF TECHNICAL CHANGE   7

2   Division of labour and economic theory   9
   2.1   Introduction   9
   2.2   Major classical contributions   10
   2.3   The role of the market   21
   2.4   Division of labour and social welfare   27
   2.5   Conclusions   30

3   Division of labour and technical change   33
   3.1   Introduction   33
   3.2   An endogenous view of technical change   35
   3.3   Division of labour and increasing returns   37
   3.4   Dynamic increasing returns and equilibrium theory . . .   48

3.5   Conclusions   57

II   FORMAL REPRESENTATIONS OF THE PROCESS OF DIVISION OF LABOUR   59

4   Stochastic models of division of labour   61
   4.1   Introduction   61
   4.2   Stochastic processes in economics   62
   4.3   Division of labour as a stochastic process   68
   4.4   Conclusions   84

5   Division of labour and progress functions   87
   5.1   Introduction   87
   5.2   The progress function theory   88
   5.3   The innovative process   96
   5.4   'The division of labour depends on the division of labour'   99
   5.5   Conclusions   108

III   IMPLICATIONS FOR THE THEORY OF THE FIRM AND MARKET FORMS   111

6   Division of labour and theory of the firm   113
   6.1   Introduction   113
   6.2   Division of labour and market structure   114
   6.3   Division of labour and the role of the firm   123
   6.4   Conclusions   130

7   Concluding remarks   133

Appendix A   141

Appendix B   147

Bibliography   153

List of figures

3.1 Productivity growth under dynamic increasing
    returns   43
3.2 A graphical representation of the classical
    'postulates'   45
3.3 Average costs under dynamic increasing returns   46
3.4 The division of labour and the extent of the
    market: expansion and contraction paths   48
3.5 Marshall's 'normal' supply curve under
    increasing returns   54
3.6 Equilibrium of demand and supply under static
    increasing returns   56

4.1 Relationships between α, β and i   79

5.1 Density function of a Pareto distribution for
    different values of k   94

6.1 Stigler's diagram 120
6.2 The lowering of the average cost curve 122

B.1 Engel's curves 148

List of tables

4.1 Pioneering works in stochastic models of economic processes 64

4.2 Returns to adopting A or B 66

1 Introduction

The purpose of this research† is to revive the classical division-of-labour theory in an attempt to provide an adequate explanation of the process of technical change, considered as one of the key factors of endogenous economic growth.

The reason for carrying out this sort of investigation is two-fold.

- Over the last few years the economic analysis of technical change has grown apace, and it appears to be a particularly appropriate time to give such a contribution.

- There are still many questions, especially of a conceptual and theoretical nature, to which economics has to answer as far as the *origin* and the *development* of technical change is con-

---

†This book is based on the author's Ph.D. thesis presented in January 1990. She is grateful to her former supervisor, Ian Steedman, who provided generous advice and constant guidance while she was working on her thesis; without his acute perception of logical weakness and willingness to discuss difficulties, she doubts whether this book would have appeared at all. She is also grateful to Alessandro Roncaglia, who went patiently through several drafts, served as a sounding board for the testing of ideas, and forced her to more rigorous thinking and clearer expression.

At various stages she has benefited from comments by R.Arena, S.Biasco, E.Matzner, S.Metcalfe, F.Papangelou, C.Sardoni, B.Schefold, J.Steindl, P.Swann and P.Sylos Labini. The usual disclaimer applies.

cerned. This book aims to give a contribution specifically in that direction.[1]

The economic analysis of technical change, it need hardly be said, is not a straightforward matter. The familiar tools of equilibrium economics are not suited to analyse the disequilibrium processes by which new technologies are generated, improved and absorbed into the economic structures. For this reason the concepts on which the work is built are not the ones to which economists are nowadays most accustomed, although, at the same time, they are not new — their origin being traced back to the works of the classical economists.

It is the purpose of Chapter 2 to reconsider the classical division-of-labour theory, drawing attention to the two major contributions by Adam Smith and Charles Babbage. Meanwhile, it is important to stress that, in this context, we are not interested in the history of the classical idea of division of labour *per se* [cf., for this purpose, CORSI(1983) and GROENEWEGEN(1987)]. On the contrary, we wish to take this idea from the original context to a theoretical stage at which, in our view, it can be developed, independently of what has actually happened to it through time.

According to the classical economists the concept of division of labour has many dimensions. First of all, we must distinguish two different kinds of division of labour: 1) the *social division of labour* or the division of society into occupation and professions, and 2) the *industrial division of labour*, which refers to the different tasks performed within a process of production. Whereas traditional market theory usually refers to the social division of labour — as a precondition of the existence of exchange — and considers it as a result of

---

[1]In recent years a major topic of concern has been the impact that new microelectronic or information technology will have on national economies [see, for example, BERTING(1980) and relative bibliography]. In this sort of discussion it is usually forgotten that the impact is at the end of a long chain of economic decision-making involving the generation and implementation of new technology. To consider only the impact would suggest that the new technology arrives as a *deus ex machina*, whereas the processes of selection and rejection of technologies do actually shape the nature of new technologies coming forth, the rate at which they arise, and the origin of the new technologies [cf. SAHAL(1981)]. For an idea of the directions which the economics of technical change is taking, see, for example, STONEMAN(1983) and DOSI(1988).

natural or innate differences between individuals, our investigation will concentrate on the industrial division of labour, considered as the linch-pin of productivity performance. In both its forms, that of intra-firm differentiation of labour[2] and that of inter-firm specialization of production, the industrial division of labour has, in our view, the following economic consequences.

- It allows for a faster execution of the various productive operations and, above all, a better organization of the working process as a whole, including the elimination of unnecessary operations.

- It points to a systematic way of studying and organizing the labour process, which makes it possible to assign all the workers specifically endowed with the required skills to the single simple operations, improving performance and reducing costs of production [Babbage's principle of economy of skill].

- It makes possible the substitution of routine and repetitive human works by machinery.[3]

In all these ways it implies increasing productivity. Moreover, it implies a flow of innovations of various kinds (organizational, managerial, technical, etc.), which are stimulated by the increasing rationalization of the productive process. The introduction of these innovations is bounded by the structural characteristics of the economic system (existing professions and trades, as well as prevailing technologies). However, this 'boundary' tends to shift through time, in so far as economic progress brings into being new products and new methods of production.

We must define what we mean by *technical change*. Here, technical change is understood in a very wide sense as the long term increase in

---

[2] As far as the intra-firm differentiation of labour is concerned, it is important to distinguish between the *subdivision of labour* — i.e. the progressive simplification of the individual activities composing the working process — and the *displacement of labour*, which refers to the substitution of machines for workers, once the working activity has been simplified enough to be performed automatically.

[3] We refer to dynamic substitution, in the sense that it can only be the result of technological or organizational changes. It differs therefore from static substitution which takes place between labour and capital goods, *given* technology and the organization of the productive process.

product per man, at a given degree of utilization of labour resources. It is therefore considered, essentially, as a process of *improvement in production practice*, in which the whole society is, to a greater or lesser extent, involved.[4]

It will be clear that, as they are conceived here, increasing division of labour and technical change are intimately related: they both refer to an increasing-returns-to-scale process of knowledge-driven economic growth, in which interdependence and feedback between different stages of development are extremely important for explaining the dynamics of the process.

It is very often claimed that technical change cannot be properly modelled because of the difficulty of analysing its determinants and predicting its direction.[5] For this reason we explicitly analyse some methodological problems implicit in our approach.[6]

In our view, the process of 'division of labour–technical change' presents some specific characteristics:

- it is an endogenous process affected by various economic factors (such as, potential demand, real wages, current and/or expected profits, degree of utilized capacity — see Ch.3);

---

[4] As in DOSI(1984), we understand technology, in a wide sense too, as 'a set of pieces of knowledge, both directly "practical" (related to concrete problems and devices) and "theoretical" (but practically applicable although not necessarily already applied), know-how, methods, procedures, experience of successes and failures and also, of course, physical devices and equipment'(p.14).

[5] This reason is, for example, adduced to justify the 'residual' empirical approach. Cf. KENNEDY–THIRLWALL(1972): 'The best that can be done is to measure technical change by its effects, such as its impact on the growth of national income, or on the growth of factor productivity not accounted for by other inputs, leaving technical change as a residual. (..) This approach, of course, has the distinct disadvantage of not being able to separate technical change from other inputs not specified, and possibly of confusing advances in knowledge with other factors which may raise productivity, but *there seems to be no alternative*'(p.13; our italics).

[6] *Nota bene*: We do not deal with the empirical detail of technical change — such detail can be found, for instance, in FREEMAN(1982) and SAHAL(1981). The emphasis on theoretical analysis reflects a view that one needs theory before empirical investigation, and that it is largely in the theoretical field that the major advances in the economics of technical change must be made [cf. PASINETTI(1981) and NELSON–WINTER(1982)].

- it takes place through time in a discontinuous manner and follows a path which is not predictable;

- previous organizational and technical changes influence the outcome of the process *via* self-reinforcing mechanisms [e.g. accumulation of knowledge due to improvements by practice].

Moreover it requires analyses at two separate levels: that of the capacity of firms to generate a particular technological performance (micro level); and that of the interaction between firms within a market environment in which their technological differences are resolved into changes of quantities and prices (macro level). To deal with these features of the process of change we draw, at micro level [Ch.4], on stochastic modelling (Markov models) and, at macro level [Ch.5], on a deterministic model — a revised version of the progress function, which we merge with Sraffa's model to consider the industrial operations as an interrelated whole.

The formal representations of the process of 'division of labour–technical change' allow us to describe the emergence of dynamic economies of scale and to study their impact in terms of economic growth. In brief, we show that:

- despite its random nature, the division of labour gives rise to a 'balanced' sequence of organizational and technical changes and, in this way, causes a steady increase of productivity [see Ch.4];

- as an effect of the innovations generated by the process of division of labour, variations in production prices are influenced by changes in output which occur in *all* industries linked by using the same means of production [see Ch.5].

Our analysis emphasizes the role of the firm as decision-unit and paves the way to the study of the implications of the division of labour in terms of theory of the firm and market structure. In our view, it is extremely important, in that perspective, to evaluate the effects of innovations on the size of the firm. In Ch.6 — after having introduced, in accordance with the classical viewpoint, a view of competition as rivalry between producers — we analyse the determinants of firm size and we stress, also in this context, the unpredictability of the outcome: many alternatives are possible according to the combination of the economic factors which influence the relationship between division of labour and size of the firm.

The topics treated in Chapters 4, 5 and 6 allow us to connect our analysis to several 'heterodox' contributions, which deserve particular attention. As far as the stochastic approach is concerned, we have considered in detail Arthur's model of competing technologies [see ARTHUR (1983), (1987), (1988)]. In comparison with this model, our models are extremely elementary, and do not allow general considerations about 'potential non-superiority' or 'structural rigidity' of the process of increasing returns. However, as in Arthur's case, our models are path-dependent and indeed they prove to be very similar to two classes of models which ARTHUR(1987) names 'allocation processes' and 'recontracting processes'.[7] As far as the 'macro' model presented in Ch.5 is concerned, we mainly wish to connect our analysis with the Sraffian attempt to reconstruct classical economics [see RONCAGLIA(1978) and relative bibliography]. Moreover, with respect to theory of the firm and market form we give large space to a 'behavioural' and 'managerial' view of the nature of the firm. Finally, it should be stressed that the whole plan of this book has been largely influenced by Steindl's approach to the analysis of technical progress [see STEINDL(1965),(1974) and (1980)].

---

[7]Both these classes of dynamic models are of a 'self-reinforcing' type. In Arthur's words: 'Self-reinforcement goes under different labels in different parts of economics: increasing returns; cumulative causation; deviation–amplifying mutual causal processes; virtuous and vicious circles; threshold effects; non-convexity. The sources vary. But usually self-reinforcing mechanisms are variants of or derive from four generic sources: large set-up or fixed costs (which give the advantage of falling unit costs to increased output); learning effects (which act to improve products or lower their cost as their prevalence increases); coordination effects (which confer advantages to "going along" with other economic agents taking similar action); and adaptive expectations (where increased prevalence on the market enhances beliefs of further prevalence).'[ARTHUR(1987), p.2].

PART I
THE CLASSICAL
CONCEPTUALIZATION OF
TECHNICAL CHANGE

2 Division of labour and economic theory

2.1 Introduction

The purpose of this part of the work is to provide the foundations of the following analysis, introducing what we name 'the classical conceptualization of technical change', on the basis of the classical division-of-labour theory.

The concept of division of labour had been familiar to economic reasoning for centuries — SCHUMPETER(1954) refers to it as 'this eternal commonplace of economics'(p.56). Many of the major Greek philosophers discussed aspects of the division of labour in their writings, particularly Plato and Xenophon [see FOLEY(1974), McNULTY (1975)]. Towards the end of the 17th century, economic literature [e.g. PETTY (1671)], rediscovered the concept and began to analyse the more modern manufacturing form, linking it with productivity growth, cost reduction and increased international competiveness, and associating its scope with the more extensive markets from increased urbanization [see GROENEWEGEN(1987) and relative references]. The analysis underwent further qualitative change in the 18th century, especially after Adam Smith had considered it 'practically the only factor of economic progress' [SCHUMPETER(1954), p.187]; it retained a varying, but often very prominent place in 19th century writings (particularly those of Senior, Babbage, Marx and

J.S.Mill), but disappeared as a major topic from economic texts during the first half of the 20th century, mainly because of the difficulty of modern equilibrium analysis to come to grips with the dynamic features of the division of labour. Only from the 1950s onwards, did the return of economic growth as an important part of the economist's research programme [and earlier the work of YOUNG(1928)] restore interest in the division of labour, as the organising principle of production.

It is therefore the time (in our view) to re-discuss the different dimensions of the concept: this is the aim of the first part of the book. In this chapter, our first purpose is to introduce the reader to the classical division-of-labour theory, drawing attention to the two major contributions by Adam Smith and Charles Babbage — without denying, nevertheless, the relevance of other contributions (e.g. by Marx or by J.S.Mill) to which we will often refer.

The importance of Smith's treatment of the division of labour is fully recognized: as BÜCHER(1907) stresses, the 'popularity [of the concept of division of labour] is indeed due in no small measure to the external circumstance that it is presented in the first chapter of Book I of his classical work [the *Wealth of Nations*], where it could not escape even to the legion of those who merely "read at" books'(p.283). However, Babbage's discussion, presented in his *On the Economy of Machinery and Manufactures*, reviews the Smithian analysis in the light of the factory system and, in our view, gives an important contribution to our understanding of the social and economic effects of the industrial division of labour [see CORSI(1984), (1986)].

In what follows, we first survey the works of these two authors and then we devote our analysis to the discussion of two specific topics: 1)the role of the market in the process of division of labour, and 2)the link between division of labour and social welfare.

2.2   Major classical contributions

2.2.1   Adam Smith

The analysis of the division of labour is the starting point of Adam Smith's *Inquiry into the Nature and Causes of the Wealth of the Na-*

tions, and provides the foundation for his model of economic development.[1]

According to Smith, the division of labour is the organizing principle of production. Moreover, it may be regarded as the main determinant of productivity performance:

> The greatest improvement in the productive powers of labour, and the greater part of the skill, dexterity, and judgment with which it is any where directed, or applied, seem to have been the effects of the division of labour. [SMITH(1776), p.13]

In Chapter 1 of Book I, Smith describes different kinds of division of labour: the *social division of labour*, or the division of society into occupations and professions, and the *industrial division of labour*, which refers to the different tasks performed within a process of production. In its turn, the latter manifests itself in two ways: *inter-firm specialization of production* and *intra-firm differentiation of labour*.

Smith illustrates each process by industrial examples and from them deduces the characteristics of the various kinds of division of labour. There is first the celebrated example of the pin manufacture, which refers to the intra-firm differentiation of labour. With the ordinary workman who is not particularly adept at this special production, Smith contrasts the factory in which a considerable number of workmen with divided labour produce similar commodities. 'One man draws out the wire; another straights it; a third cuts it; a fourth points it; a fifth grinds it at the top for receiving the head; to make the head requires two or three distinct operations, (..)'(p.15); in this way there result, up to the completion of the pin, eighteen distinct operations, each of which can be transferred to a partial worker. Smith

---

[1]Referring to the growth model developed for Book I, Ch.3 of the *Wealth of Nations* by HICKS(1965), the rate of growth of output in the economy depends, according to Smith, on three variables: the proportion of productive labour in the total labour supply (the saving ratio), the wage rate, and the level of labour productivity (product per capita). According to GROENEWEGEN(1977) Smith seems to have believed that the scope for important increases in the proportion of the labour force devoted to productive activities was limited. Thus, given the real wage, a substantial growth rate depends exclusively on rising productivity, through extensions of the division of labour.

finds that in such a co-operating group of workers the output of each individual, as compared with that of the labourer working separately and producing the whole product, is increased a hundred, indeed a thousandfold.

This example has been repeated even to weariness; it has become, in general, the classic type of division of labour. Many economists, apparently, can conceive of it only in this one form, the form of a manufacture in which the total labour necessary to the production of the ware is divided into as many simple operations as possible, carried on simultaneously by different people in the same establishment.

But Adam Smith has not confined himself to this example. On the one hand, as far as the social division of labour is concerned, Smith considers the instance of the woollen manufacture. In a 'rude' state of the society, he argues, the production of woollen cloth is the work of one man, from the procuring of the raw material till it is ready for use; in every 'improved' society, on the contrary, 'the farmer is generally nothing but a farmer; the manufacturer nothing but a man-ufacturer'(p.16). On the other hand, to illustrate the inter-firm specialization of production, Smith compares three smiths: 'a common smith, who though accustomed to handle the hammer, has never been accustomed to make nails'; a second smith 'who has been accustomed to make nails', but has not this as his sole or principal occupation; and finally a nail-smith who has never been accustomed to any other occupation (pp.18). He finds that if all three make nails for a definite period the work done increases according as the workman limits himself to the production of one product. Clearly, Smith conceives the whole business of a smith who originally makes horseshoes, spades, etc., as well as nails, as the subject of the process of division. From this comprehensive department of production a line of production is separated, and taken over by a special workman, the nail-smith, while the remaining products continue to form part of the ordinary smith's work. The articles formerly produced jointly in the one business of the smith are henceforth manufactured in two different businesses. In the place of one firm there are now two, and each provides for an individual a separate employment.

Smith ascribes to the various forms of industrial division of labour the same effects: 1) increased dexterity of the workman, 2) saving of time, and 3) the invention of machinery which facilitates labour.[2] Since the division of labour is more easily carried out in manufactures, it is in the manufacturing sector that costs would decline and it is this sector of the economy, therefore, that is linked with increasing returns.[3] These consequences of the division of labour in turn are responsible for the tremendous rise in living standards experienced by civilised nations, 'or that universal opulence which extends itself to the lowest ranks of the people'(p.22).

Chapters 2 and 3 of Book I, and the introduction to Book II discuss both the prerequisites for and the constraints on the division of labour.according to Smith, the division of labour 'is not originally the effect of any human wisdom, which foresees and intends that general opulence to which it gives occasion'; it arises, mainly, from a human 'propensity to truck and barter, and exchange one thing for another' (p.25).[4] Division of labour — considered as the linch-pin of productivity performance — is therefore only possible in an exchange economy, and hence is limited by 'the extent of the market': an expansion of the market (i.e. of the potential demand for final output) increases the division of labour which can promote, through a cost reduction, the growth of production and a subsequent expansion of the market.

A final requirement for the division of labour is given in the intro-

---

[2]MARGLIN(1974) has criticized the three grounds on which Smith bases his assertion about the high productivity of the division of labour, attributing this, alternatively to the introduction of a 'discipline cum supervision' by the factory employer. LANDES(1986) has provided a very convincing reply to Marglin's arguments, and has 'rehabilitated' Smith's point of view.

[3]According to Smith, the division of labour in agriculture has a more limited scope than in manufacturing, so that the increase in productivity tends to be slower than in the other sector. However, this is very different from Ricardo's idea of long-run predominance of diminishing returns in agriculture. Indeed, Smith distinguishes two categories of agricultural products — vegetables and cattle — and argues that only the second category is subject to a sort of tendency toward diminishing returns [cf. SMITH(1776), p.259].

[4]ARROW(1979) criticizes Adam Smith for regarding exchange as the only means whereby the division of labour can be originated and the co-ordination of different kinds of work achieved.he argues that self-interest and market type co-operation can be effective only in the presence of some 'ethical codes' and stress the risk of imperfect information and mistrust as consequences of the specialization of experience. Arrow seems to forget the existence of Smith's *Theory of Moral Sentiments*!

duction of Book II, thereby linking the analysis of capital to that of the division of labour. In the second paragraph of this introduction Smith demonstrates that a prior accumulation of capital must exist when the division of labour is practised, in order to maintain the worker, 'and to supply him with the materials and tools of his work till such time' that the production process has been completed and the output has been sold (p.276). Later it is argued that the extent of the division of labour is in this way limited by the accumulation of capital and, in addition, that such accumulation encourages further division of labour because the capitalist wants to secure a maximum return for his advances (p.277). The division of labour and the accumulation of capital are therefore strongly interrelated.[5]

2.2.2   Charles Babbage

Charles Babbage's discussion of the division of labour, in his *On the Economy of Machinery and Manufactures* concentrates mainly on the industrial division of labour applied to each individual working processes.

The main purpose of Babbage's interest in the division of labour is to identify rational solutions to minimize costs of production. In chapter XIX, after having defined his point of view on the origin of the division of labour as the organizing principle of production, Babbage analyses the advantages related to this kind of organization and usually seen as factors of increasing productivity. The common characteristic of all these factors is the *reduction of necessary working time* (i.e. the direct or indirect labour content of one unit of output). This, with a given amount of labour time employed, makes it possible to increase the amount of goods produced. Moreover, the increasing specialization of operations reduces apprenticeship time, i.e., less time is needed for instructing each individual worker for his specific tasks. At the same time there is also a reduction in the amount of wasted

---

[5]ELTIS(1975) stresses that the Smithian model of economic growth attributes overwhelming importance to the rate of capital accumulation, which is a function of the ratio of productive to unproductive employment. He argues that, according to Smith, fixed capital rises as the economy grows; thus there is upward or downward pressure on profits dependent on the relative growth rates of capital and output.

material. When the worker performs only a specific operation, he puts specific muscular strength and attention to use; and this, after a variable period of training, makes it possible to obtain the desired result with maximum efficiency. Obviously, when the worker performs many kinds of operations within a single day, there will be waste of time, because of the large amount of time necessary for adapting to the new operation, when the worker has to shift from one kind of operation to another.

The same reasoning holds for the time necessary to prepare instruments and machines for work. Less time is required if the instruments and machines are prepared once and then always used for the same operation. When the worker performs the same operation, with the same instrument, we have the condition for continuous improvement both in the manual execution of the operation and in the instruments.

The principle of economy of skill Smith and other economists after him, had already made these observations starting from the existence of a certain kind of division of labour already operating within the manufacturing system. But Babbage starts by looking for rational patterns that allow for the refinement of the division of labour, optimizing its results in terms of increasing productivity. According to Babbage, in order to identify rational patterns in the division of labour, we need quantitative analysis, which allows one to establish the exact amount of strength and skill required by any specific operation.

Using quantitative examples, Babbage introduces the following principle of economy of skill[6]:

That the master manufacturer, by dividing the work to be executed into different processes, each requiring different degrees of skill or of force, can purchase exactly that precise quantity of both which is necessary for each process;

---

[6]This is just the economic application of a more general principle:'One of the most important processes in all inquiry is to divide the subject to be considered into as many different questions as it will admit of, and then to examine each separately; or, in other words, to suppose that each single cause successively varies, while all others remain constant'[BABBAGE(1851), p.4]

whereas, if the whole work were executed by one workman, that person must possess sufficient skill to perform
the most difficult, and sufficient strength to execute the
most laborious, of the operations into which the art is divided. [BABBAGE(1832), pp.175-6].[7]

According to Babbage, this principle is the basis for obtaining the
greatest advantages from the division of labour. Indeed, this principle has a general, decisive relevance: it impressed later economists,
including J.S.Mill[8], Marx[9] and Marshall[10], and it reappears in Taylor's method of the scientific division of labour.

[7]In a footnote Babbage argues that he has taken this principle from Melchiorre
Gioja, *Nuovo Prospetto delle Scienze Economiche*, G.Pirotta, Milano, 1815. For a
more detailed analysis of the linkages between Babbage's and Gioja's works, see
SCAZZIERI(1981),pp.55-71.

[8]In describing the economic consequences of the division of labour, J.S.Mill argues that the 'greatest advantage (next to the dexterity of the workmen) derived
from the minute division of labour (..)is one not mentioned by Adam Smith , but to
which attention has been drawn by Mr.Babbage; the more economical distribution
of labour, by classing the workpeople according to their capacity' [MILL(1848),
p.129].In other words, for Mill, as for Babbage, the division of labour mainly provides a rational solution to minimize the costs of production. Far from being a
process of adaptation of the tasks of labour to the variety of human vocations, the
division of labour is conceived by Mill as the adaptation of individual powers to the
tasks to be performed, as the continued differentiation of the one and of the other.

[9]Marx quoted what we may call 'the first principle of Babbage' in the first volume
of *Capital*, when he analyses the 'organic manufacture' [cf. MARX(1867),p.469n.].
However, as far as his analysis of the collective worker is concerned, Marx is influenced by Andrew Ure more than by Babbage:

Dr. Ure, in his apotheosis of large-scale industry, brings out
the peculiar character of manufacture more sharply than previous
economists, who did not have his polemical interest in the matter,
and more sharply even than his contemporaries — for instance Babbage, who, although much his superior in mathematics and mechanics,
treated large-scale industry from the standpoint of manufacture alone
(p.470n.).

In the light of our interpretation of Charles Babbage's works, Marx is right only
when he stresses the scientific superiority of Charles Babbage in comparison with
Andrew Ure [cf.CORSI(1983), pp.100-13].

[10]Marshall, in his *Industry and Trade*(1919) sees American standardized production as an 'unprecedented' application of 'Babbage's great principle of economical
production'(p.149). Moreover, discussing the principles of scientific management

In order to clarify this principle, Babbage uses a pin-making example, similar to the Smithian one.[11] He presents a table of the time required by each process, and its cost, as well as the wage of the people who are confined solely to a single process. According to Babbage, this kind of study shows clearly that, if the worker paid with the maximum wage accomplished all the phases of the working process, a part of his working time would be wasted: in fact, even if his productivity were equal to the productivity of the worker specialized in the single operation, the cost would be twice as much, because of the higher wage paid to the 'general' worker in comparison with the 'partial' worker.

Dynamic substitution Babbage analyses the division of both physical and mental labour. His analysis of working methods concerns the factors which concur in obtaining the maximum effect in each working operation (e.g. in the case of the physical labour, the weight of the arm, the weight of the instrument and the frequency of each operation) and the study of the many degrees of skill required by each operation. As a result of these studies the working process is divided into its primitive elements, which can then be rearranged into the effective working process. This method would later constitute the foundation of the so-called 'scientific division of labour', developed by Winslow Taylor. But Babbage's view is, in a sense, much more sophisticated than Taylor's. In fact, according to Babbage, identifying the primitive operations which make up the working process allows us to identify the possibilities of replacing any single simple operation with certain instruments or machines. According to the above mentioned principle of economy of skill, when the working process is considered as a series of specific operations, it becomes possible to assign all the workers specifically endowed with the requisite skills to the single simple operation, improving the performance and reducing

---

(Book II) he argues that 'One of the chief ideas of Scientific Management was worked out a considerable way by Babbage (..);and, for good reasons, he took as his chief illustration the common task of shovelling earth, which Taylor was to use for the same purpose later on'(p.376).

[11]In his *The Exposition of 1851*, Babbage speaks about two men engaged in shovelling earth (pp.3-4).

costs of production.

However, at the same time, Babbage argues that the division of mental as well as physical labour can be sufficiently refined to enable the capitalist to substitute machinery for the routine and repetitive processes, lowering costs even further.[12]

This show that Babbage does not confine himself to analysing the system of manufactures. Actually, as we have tried to show, Babbage not only traces, in his *On the Economy of Machinery and Manufactures*, both the causes and the consequences of applying machinery 'to supersede the skill and power of the human arm'; but he especially promotes a new industrial organization of both mental and physical labour, so that workers can be substituted by machinery, for the routine and repetitive processes. Babbage sees this 'cooperative substitution', of workers by machinery as the main factor of increasing productivity. Moreover he believes that the progressive specialization of productive functions and the introduction of very sophisticated machines will set the human creative imagination free for inventing new machines and new products. Referring to this point, Babbage seems to agree with Adam Smith, who attributes 'capacity to invent' in a technically progressive society only to 'philosophers or men of speculation, whose trade it is not to do anything but to observe every thing; and who, upon that account are often capable of combining together the powers of the most distant and dissimilar objects'[SMITH(1776),p.21].

The principle of numerical proportions Babbage — like Marx and Mill later — connects the intra-firm division of labour and the process of industrial concentration. In his chapter 'On the causes and consequences of large factories' Babbage enumerates the conditions which give rise to increasing returns to scale and lower prices for manufactured articles [J.S. Mill's *Principles* contains page-length quotations from this section of *On Manufactures*].

Following Smith, Babbage recognizes that 'the division of labour cannot be successfully practiced unless there exists a great demand

---

[12]As an instance of this, and a very relevant one from the contemporary point of view, we can consider the so-called 'computing engines' develop by Babbage himself.

for its produce', and he adds that this in turn 'requires a large capital to be employed in those arts in which it is used'(p.201):

> The inducement to contrive machines for any process of manufacture increases with demand for the article; and the introduction of machinery, on the other hand, tends to increase the quantity produced, and to lead to the establishment of large factories(..). Hence arises one cause of the great size of manufacturing establishments, which have increased with the progress of civilization (pp.213-14).

Babbage apparently feels that as long as the division of labour and demand are extended, there is no limit to the size of the firm. With regard to this topic, he introduces the following *principle of numerical proportions*:

> When the number of processes into which it is most advantageous to divide it, and the number of individuals to be employed in it, are ascertained, then all factories which do not employ a direct multiple of this latter number, will produce the article at a greater cost (p.212).

Let us note that in reaching this conclusion Babbage implicitly refers to the production of a specified good by a number of competing firms. If we assume that the production of any commodity is undertaken not by one firm but by many firms, each of which specializes in some activity, the conclusions may be different. When activities, although complementary, are in general not similar, firms will tend to expand selectively the activities, in which, relative to competitors, they have a comparative advantage, and to rely, to an increasing extent, on sales to or purchases from other businesses [see Ch.6].

Babbage discusses several other reasons for the cost advantages of large firms. Among the more interesting are the following:

- large firms may generate sufficient by-products to allow for their processing and sale;

- a large established firm has a name that customers trust, thus lowering information costs; and its financial power makes those dissatisfied with its products less likely to take legal action against it;

- large manufactures can, with their capital, undertake the research necessary to produce new products and lower the cost of existing ones [BABBAGE(1832), pp.217-24].

Babbage feels that, despite the concentration of capital, monopoly can be avoided if consumers have adequate product information[13] and entry is not restricted:

If the supply, or present stock in hand, be entirely in the possession of one person, he will naturally endeavour to put such a price upon it as shall produce by its sale the greatest quantity of money; but he will be guided in this estimate of the price at which he will sell, both by the knowledge that increased price will cause a diminished consumption, and by the desire to realize his profit before a new supply shall reach the market from some other quarter (p.143).

Competition takes the form of introducing new products, production processes, and organizational techniques. Any monopoly rents obtained within this environment are usually temporary in nature due to the dynamic forces of innovation. Implicit in this discussion is the assumption that free entry is normally present and that any attempt to raise prices artificially would bring new firms into the market [see Ch.6].

---

[13] According to ROMANO(1982), Babbage may have been the first writer to include information costs as an element of price and to explain the connection between these costs and price dispersion. He labels the cost to the consumer of obtaining information about a product a 'verification cost' and in his book gives a number of examples where difficulties in obtaining product and price information raise costs and lead to a greater dispersion of prices among sellers in a competitive market.

2.3 The role of the market

2.3.1 'The division of labour is limited by the extent of the market'

The survey presented in the previous section gives us the opportunity of pointing out the main characteristics of the classical division-of-labour theory.

According to the classical point of view, we must distinguish three different kinds of division of labour: 1)the social division of labour, 2)the intra-firm differentiation of labour and 3)the inter-firm specialization of production. In its turn, the second manifests itself in two forms: subdivision of labour and displacement of labour.[14] The former consists in the progressive simplification of the individual activities composing the working process; the latter refers to the substitution of machines for workers, once the working activity has been simplified enough to be performed automatically.

All these different kinds of division of labour have something in common: they are all processes in the evolution of an exchange economy in which an economic task is transferred from the one worker hitherto performing it to several workers, the transfer being so made that each of these performs but a separate part of the previous work.

In the case of the displacement of labour, the machine usually undertakes separate movements that until then have been performed by human hands, and the only initial change is generally the transfer of the workman, who formerly performed that activity to attendance upon the machine. When newly-invented machines are introduced, that attendance may require the possession (or the acquisition through training) of a particular qualification. Nevertheless, given that the machine is a commodity and is probably produced through subdivision of labour, also in this case the work of the single worker previously employed is actually substituted by a whole group of workers performing partial activities. If we consider the whole process of production, this is equivalent to having a part of the total labour pushed back from a later to an earlier stage.

Bearing this point in mind, we can say that, according to the

---

[14]We borrow the term 'displacement of labour' from BÜCHER(1907).

classical point of view, the division of labour is always characterized by an increase in the number of workers necessary for the accomplishment of a definite job, and at the same time by a differentiation of work.

This has at least two main implications at micro and macro levels of analysis.

From a micro point of view, division of labour is always at the same time classification of labour and ranking of different activities; its result is co-operation either between workers with different skills or between workers and machinery.

From a macro viewpoint, the simultaneous increases of labour productivity and number of workers necessary for the accomplishment of a definite job stress the importance of an increase in income, as a necessary condition for the increase of the division of labour.

Let us consider more closely this second implication, i.e. the Smithian theorem that 'the division of labour is limited by the extent of the market.' As we stressed above, in Smith's discussion we can distinguish three different categories of division of labour[15]: 1) division within a firm (intra-firm differentiation of labour); 2) division between firms (inter-firm specialization of labour); 3) division between industries and/or trades (social division of labour).

Therefore, according to the context, 'the extent of the market' denotes the potential demand for final output 1) of one firm, 2) of a group of firms, 3) of the economy as a whole. Each of these three versions of the theorem would deserve a separate discussion [cf.WILLIAMS(1978)]. However, in our view, Smith's theorem rests essentially upon the following idea. If work is thought of as divided into a set of tasks, a firm which produces one item a day might have one worker doing all the tasks; if output expanded to two items, it could have two workers, each doing half the tasks; at three items, it would have three workers doing one-third of the tasks; and so on until each worker did a single task. [Since the rationale is increased productivity, the work day would get shorter, or output larger, with each division.] Obviously, the limit to this division of labour is the

---

[15]Modern economists have usually analysed the division of labour only from one of the various classical points of view. So, for example, STIGLER(1951) refers to the inter-firm specialization of production; LEIJONHUFVUD(1986) to the intra-firm differentiation of labour; ARROW(1979) to the social division of labour.

number of items produced, and this, in turn depends on the extent of the market.

The optimal market from this point of view is, in other words, a market so large that each worker can be fully employed performing a single task.

Smith seemed to think of the extent of the market in a geographic sense but, in fact, what is involved in the concept of the extent of the market is the absolute number of items relative to the number of tasks. The extent of the market, in this sense, will increase with the level of income, and rising income levels will give rise to increasing productivity, a reversal of the direction of causality usually emphasized.

The above discussion points out that the classical link between division of labour and extent of the market implies a dynamic concept of 'market'.

Traditional market theory usually considers the division of labour as a precondition of the existence of exchange. However, the concept of division of labour which prevails within this theory either refers to the *social division of labour* or is formulated on the basis of natural or innate differences between individuals.

The link between social division of labour and exchange may be accepted with the limitation that, with socially divided labour, exchange becomes necessary from the moment that producers possess all the means of production, relatively to a certain commodity; from that point on, almost every advance in the social division of labour increases the number of necessary acts of exchange.

By contrast, the view of the division of labour as a process of adaptations of the tasks of labour to the variety of human powers, can hardly be accepted from a classical perspective. Although sensitive to the differences among people which might result in comparative advantages for particular tasks, classical economists believe that 'the differences of natural talents in different men are, in reality, much less than we are aware of'[SMITH(1776), p.28) and are more often the result than the cause of the division of labour.

2.3.2   Allyn Young's discussion of the Smithian theorem

It is worth remembering that Allyn Young made the Smithian theorem the central theme of his 1928 article on increasing returns and
economic progress, arguing that this was 'one of the most illuminating
and fruitful generalisations which can be found in the whole literature
of economics'.

It is the interdependence between the expansion of the aggregate demand for goods and the expansion of aggregate output which
YOUNG(1928) explores.[16]   Young's starting point is that 'with the
division of labour a group of complex processes is transformed into a
succession of simpler processes, some of which, at least, lend themselves to the use of machinery. In the use of machinery and the adoption of indirect processes there is a further division of labour, the
economies of which are again limited by the extent of the market'
(p.530).[17]

Young focuses attention on the *creative* functions of markets and
not only on their allocative functions: 'in an inclusive view, considering the market not as the outlet for the products of a particular
industry, and therefore external to that industry, but as the outlet for
goods in general, the size of the market is determined and defined by
the volume of production. [Therefore] Adam Smith's dictum amounts
to the theorem that *the division of labour depends in large part upon
the division of labour*' (p.533; our italics).

The basic consideration underlying Young's analysis is surprisingly

---

[16]According to YOUNG(1928), 'the mechanism of increasing returns is not to be
discussed adequately by observing the effects of variations in the size of an individual firm or of a particular industry, for the progressive division and specialization
of industries is an essential part of the process by which increasing returns are re-
alized. What is required is that industrial operations be seen as an interrelated
whole'(p.539).

[17]For Young the division of labour manifests itself in two related aspects: the
growth of indirect or roundabout methods of production and specialization among
industries. 'The principal economies of the division of labour, in its modern forms,'
— Young says — 'are the economies which are to be had by using labour in roundabout or indirect ways'; however 'certain roundabout methods are fairly sure to
become feasible and economical when their advantages can be spread over the output of the whole industry.'(p.539).

similar to that underlying Say's Law.[18] If one takes an all-inclusive view of the economic process, economic activity ultimately consists of the exchange of goods for goods; this means that every increase in the supply of commodities enlarges, at least potentially, the market for other commodities. According to Young, when the demand for each commodity is elastic, 'in the special sense that a small increase in its supply will be attended by an increase in the amounts of other commodities which can be had in exchange for it'(p.534), progress is bound to be cumulative, for under such conditions an increase in the supply emanating from any particular part of the economy has a stimulating effect, and not a depressing effect, on production in other parts.[19]

Referring to this aspect of Young's presentation, Kaldor has supplied a Keynesian interpretation of this 'elasticity of demand' [see KALDOR(1972), (1985)]. In order to show how an increase in the production of a commodity may involve the generation of additional incomes which in turn generate additional demand for other commodities, according to Kaldor, we must first take into account the fact that there are two kinds of demand (and supply) in a market: a demand of 'outsiders' (namely producers and consumers) and a demand of 'merchants' (or dealers, or middlemen) who operate inside the market.

---

[18]As BAUMOL(1977) has stressed, there are several propositions which can be headed as Say's Law. We would wish to accept the following:

1. 'A community's *purchasing power* is limited by and is equal to its output, because production provides *the means* by which outputs can be purchased' (Baumol's italics; p.146);

2. 'Expenditure increases when output rises'.

Note that both propositions concern production as the source of the wealth of a nation. They tell us that output is purchasing power, but they do *not* say that all of that purchasing power will always be used to buy goods.

[19]In formalizing his model of economic progress, Young makes use of the reciprocal demand (or offer curve) which had been developed by Marshall and extended by Edgeworth to explain value in international trade. Along such a curve goods are exchanged for goods. It shows the quantity of any one good, say A, which A producers would supply to producers of another good, say B, for different amounts of B at various prices of B in terms of A. Thus the A producers' offer curve is simultaneously their supply curve for A as well as their demand curve for B. In this sense, demand and supply are inter-dependent.

What differentiates a merchant from other economic agents (such as a producer) is that his natural response to 'outside' influences is to vary the size of his stocks in the face of excess demand. The very notion of 'merchanting' activities involves therefore the assumption that there is a certain elasticity of demand for holding stocks by the traders: an elasticity which is ultimately governed by the trader's expectations concerning prices and selling opportunities in the future.

According to Kaldor, the essential element missing from Young's presentation and which can only be supplied on the basis of Keynesian economics, 'is the addition to incomes resulting from the accumulation of capital (in other words, from investment expenditure) combined with the induced character of such investment which arises more or less as a by-product of changes in the organization of production' [KALDOR(1972), p.1249]. In competitive markets, such as those for most primary products, the stocks which are essential for the functioning of the market are carried by merchants who are independent both of the producers and the consumers; it is their ability to act as a 'buffer' — to absorb stocks in the face of a short-term excess supply — which will lead to induced investment in the face of a rise in production (provided that the merchants' expectations of the future prices make it appear profitable for them to increase the value of their stocks — and not only their volume — when prices decrease in the face of excess supply). In oligopolistic markets, as in the case of many manufactures, the producers carry their own stocks and adjust their rate of production in response to changes in their sales (or in the state of their 'order book') and there will be 'induced investment' in response to an increase in demand and the associated depletion of stocks:

> Such induced investment will partly take the form of circulating capital and partly of fixed capital, in so far as the rise in current sales causes a revision of expectation of future sales. It may seem paradoxical that 'induced investment' should result from both increases in supply and increases in demand, but there is nothing necessarily inconsistent in this , provided there is asymmetry in market organisation between the two kinds of commodities, primary products and manufactures, an asymmetry which is

imposed on the system by the differing incidence of the theorem of the division of labour between industry and agriculture — a feature of life which was already noted by A.Smith [KALDOR(1972),p.1250].

2.4 Division of labour and social welfare

Until now (and in general throughout the book) we have concentrated on the economic aspects of the division of labour. However, it is important to stress that the classical economists were also very much interested in the social consequences of the division of labour. Both Smith and Babbage point out the existence of negative social consequences of the specialization of tasks induced by industrial evolution.

On the one hand, Smith, in Book V of the *Wealth of Nations*, argues that the division of labour has a harmful influence on the men who are employed in routine works, making them 'as stupid and ignorant as it is possible for a human creature to become' (p.782).[20] Smith, like Adam Ferguson in his *An Essay on the History of Civil Society* (1767)[21], invokes State action, in the form of public education, to countervail these harmful social consequences.[22]

On the other hand, Babbage points out the existence of negative social consequences of the factory system and looks for remedies in order to reconcile the various social claims stemming from the dif-

---

[20]Cf. BRAVERMAN(1974): 'While the social division of labour subdivides society, the detailed division of labour subdivides humans, and while the subdivision of society may enhance the individual and the species, the subdivision of the individual, when carried on without regard to human capabilities and needs, is a crime against the person and against humanity.'(p.73).

[21]For a discussion of the interrelationship between the ideas of these two Scottish philosophers on this subject, see HAMOVY(1968) and CORSI(1983).

[22]This 'sociological' view of the division of labour has been described as in contradiction to Smith's discussion of the economic advantages of the division of labour in Book I [see WEST(1964) and ROSENBERG(1965)]. In our view, no such contradiction is apparent from a careful reading of Smith's text. The Book I discussion of the effects of the division of labour *on the whole economic system* and the quite opposite argument in Book V that the division of labour is morally degenerating and mentally stultifying *for each worker*, are not only consistent, but are both necessary to explain the significance of the division of labour for the process of economic development.

ferent groups into which society is divided because of the division of labour. Babbage is particularly aware that the differentiation of labour and the wide introduction of machinery cause strong social contrasts, followed by the workers' resistance to any innovation.

As a remedy to this situation, he suggests the institution of a 'New System of Manufacturing' characterized by a profit-sharing or even a cooperative organization of production. He argues in particular that 'if, in every large establishment the mode of payment could be so arranged, that every person employed should derive advantage from the success of the whole; and that the profits of each individual should advance, as the factory itself produced profit, without the necessity of making any change in the wages'(p.251), then the worker would approve every technological innovation. Each worker should earn a basic wage and the rest of his income should come out as a percentage of total profits. Babbage goes so far as to consider the possibility of a system in which decisions on wages, innovations and dismissals (or hirings) involve the participation of workers. The practicability of such a project depends, of course, on the possibility of identifying social agents who want to put it into effect.[23] According to Babbage:

> It would be difficult to prevail on the large capitalist to enter upon any system, which would change the division of the profits arising from the employment of his capital in setting skill and labour in action; any alteration, therefore, must be expected rather from the small capitalist, or from the higher class of workmen, who combine the two characters; and to these classes, whose welfare will be first affected, the change is most important (p.254).

It would be a mistake to interpret this emphasis on co-operation

---

[23] J.S.Mill stresses 'the great merit' of Babbage in 'having pointed out the practicability and the advantage of extending the principle [of co-operation between employers and workers] to manufacturing industry generally' (MILL(1848), p.766). However, according to Mill,'the form of association, which if mankind continue to improve, must be expected in the end to predominate, is not that which can exist between a capitalist as chief, and workpeople without a voice in the management, but the association of the labourers themselves on terms of equality, collectively owning the capital with which they carry on their operations, and working under managers elected and removable by themselves.'(p.773).

as a contradictory point within the classical division-of-labour theory. On the contrary, the above quotations give us the opportunity to highlight the classical economists' ideas about the co-operative nature of the division of labour: co-operation among workers and between workers and machines as far as the single productive process is concerned; and co-operation between workers and capitalists as far as the more general organization of production is concerned.

Such a belief is shown not only by the fact that J.S.Mill discusses the division of labour as one aspect of the more general principle of co-operation[24], but also by the attention devoted to the principle of division of labour by radical economists within the Ricardian tradition (e.g., Thomas Hodgskin and William Thompson).[25] Indeed, the following extracts from Hodgskin's *Popular Political Economy* well represent, even if in extremestic form, the classical view about the social impact of the division of labour.

As the world grows older, and as men increase and multiply, there is a *constant, natural,* and *necessary* tendency to an increase in their *knowledge,* and consequently in their *productive power* (p.95).

The dependence complained of and mourned over, therefore, is the dependence of poverty and slavery, and not the mutual dependence occasioned by division of labour. [..] We are thus compelled to fix our attention on the other cause mentioned by M.Storch, and to affirm, that

---

[24]Quoting Wakefield's edition of the *Wealth of Nations*, Mill observes : 'Co-operation is of two distinct kinds: first, such co-operation as takes place when several persons help each other in the same employment; secondly, such co-operation as takes place when several persons help each other in different employments. These may be termed Simple Co-operation and Complex Co-operation.'[MILL (1848), p.116]

[25]William Thompson was a Co-operative socialist of the school of R. Owen; Thomas Hodgskin a philosophical anarchist following the tradition of W.Godwin. In essence, their deductions from Ricardian economics are the same: if it is admitted that labour is the source of all value, then clearly all value belongs to the labour, who should receive the whole products of his work. For a more detailed discussion of the Ricardian Socialists' view of the division of labour, see CORSI(1983) and relative bibliography.

not a part, but the whole of the poverty which he and
others have attributed to division of labour, is caused by
'*vexatious regulations*'. As far as I see my way in this complicated question, I should say that division of labour is
an admirable means by which each person may *know* all
things; while to enable him to subsist, he is required to
perform only one small part of social production (pp.138-
9; Hodgskin's italics).

It is not the purpose of this work to explore the comparative advantages of co-operation and/or profit-sharing with respect to other forms
of industrial relations. However, in our view, classical economists' insights may represent a contribution to actual debates about the emergence of trade interest [vs. class interest — see STEEDMAN(1986)]
and of new forms of industrial activities [e.g. the so-called 'flexible
specialization' theorized by PIORE–SABEL(1984) and the alternative
compensation systems supported by WEITZMAN(1983)].

2.5   Conclusions

In this chapter, we have become acquainted with four different kinds
of economic process falling under the common heading of division
of labour [i.e., social division of labour, inter-firm specialization of
production, subdivision of labour, displacement of labour]. They can
be studied from both a historical and a theoretical perspective.

In economic history each of the four kinds of process has had a
period of preponderance [see LANDES(1969),(1986)]. Society in its
long evolution from the isolated to the social economy has always
been seeking and finding new methods of organization of labour. But
it has not, because of that, discarded the old, nor will it discard them
so long as they are still capable of being at any point advantageously
employed. This also holds for the various forms of division of labour.
None of these principles of economic organization has ceased to operate. Each continues to be active in the places where it can still assert
its force. At any time, market signals (related to actual and expected
profitabilities, to the size and rate of growth of demand and to relative
prices) indicate new opportunities for the various forms of industrial

division of labour. Moreover, so far as economic progress brings with it a higher standard of living and, in connection with this, needs of a higher order, new tasks and new professions develop in the society (e.g. means of transport, communications, etc.).

From a theoretical viewpoint, the division of labour may be considered as the main determinant of productivity performance and, hence, of economic growth. The classical economists have recognized, in our view, the fundamental interactions between increases in output and increases in the specialization of functions — including changes in technology, in the organization of production, and in all input factor proportions.

Their observationally-rooted perceptions indicate as the main advantage related to the division of labour the *reduction of necessary working time* (i.e. of the direct or indirect labour content of one unit of output). However, such an effect is obtained not only through the unceasing re-organization of the actual productive operations but also *via* a flow of innovations of various kinds (managerial, technical, etc.), which are stimulated by the increasing rationalization of the productive process. The introduction of these innovations is bounded by the structural characteristics of the economic system (existing professions and trades, as well as prevailing technologies). However, this 'boundary' tends to shift through time, in so far as economic progress brings into being new products and new methods of production.

In the following chapter, we will refer to these features of the classical division-of-labour theory to analyse the link between technical change and economic growth. This will imply the need to re-define in dynamic terms the concept of increasing returns to scale and to draw the line between our theoretical approach and the traditional equilibrium theory.

3 Division of labour and technical change

3.1 Introduction

The aim of this chapter is to analyse the link between division of labour, technical change and economic development, and to discuss the implications of adopting the classical point of view with respect to the economics of technical change.

Economists have commonly accepted that technical change is the main source of dynamism in capitalist development. But relatively few have stopped to examine in depth the origins of technical change or its consequences for the economic and social system. Most have preferred, in Rosenberg's apt description [cf. ROSENBERG(1976), (1982)], not to look 'inside the black box', but to leave that task to technologists and historians, preferring to concentrate their own efforts on *ceteris paribus* models, which relegate technical and institutional change to the role of exogenous variables.

Classical economists were generally more keen to look inside the black box. Their conceptualization of technical change, based on the theory of division of labour, not only does consider technical change as an endogenous variable, but also allows one, at the same time, to deal with dynamic increasing returns as a factor of economic growth.

As is well known, within economic analysis the term 'technical change' has been given a wide range of meanings and interpretations. As far as a 'macro' approach to this matter is concerned, many economists have used this term to refer to the effects of changes in technology, or more specifically the role of technical progress in the growth process. In this context economic studies, in general, attempt to quantify the rate of technical progress as a determinant of the growth of output, and orthodox theorists, in particular, tend to consider technical change as a shift in the production function. From a 'micro' point of view, one can use the same term in order to refer to changes in technology itself. In this context, economic studies usually deal with research and development activity, as well as with invention and the diffusion of technology.

As we have already stressed in Ch.1, technical change is here understood in a very wide sense as the long term increase in product per man, at a given degree of utilisation of labour resources. It is therefore considered, essentially, as a process of *improvement in production practice*, in which the whole society is, to a greater or lesser extent, involved.

According to the classical point of view, productivity improvement is mainly due to increased division of labour. This does not mean that increased operative skills are the only cause of improvement through experience.On the contrary, the classical concept of division of labour implies many causes of increasing productivity, e.g. increased management efficiency in work co-ordination, introduction of superior methods of production, increased training, etc.

It is clear that, subject to this qualification, increasing division of labour and technical change, are intimately related: they both refer to an increasing-returns-to-scale process of knowledge-driven economic growth, in which interdependence and feedback between different stages of development are extremely important for explaining the dynamics of the process.

[The analysis of the theoretical implications of adopting the classical concept of technical change will be further developed in Part III, with reference to market forms and the theory of the firm.]

3.2   An endogenous view of technical change

The adoption of the classical point of view (described in Ch.2) gives
the economic analysis of technical change two distinctive features:
1) technical change is considered as an endogenous process — both
its origin and its development are linked by a mutual relationship to
economic factors; 2) macro- and micro-perspectives are combined in
a unified approach which emphasizes the role of technical change as
a factor of economic growth.

   1) Whereas much economic theory regards technical change as an
exogenous process (despite its decisive role in economic development),
according to the classical viewpoint, technical change is an endogenous process affected by three economic conditions. First of all, it
depends on the 'extent of the market' — to use Adam Smith's expression — which represents the general condition of the increasing
division of labour and, hence, of technical change. The expansion of
the market brings into being new activities and promotes the introduction of both new 'capital' goods and new consumption goods. The
product innovations often satisfy needs of a higher order and therefore presuppose an increase in the average 'per capita' income. The
process innovations improve the productive performance and bring
about a further augmentation of output. From both sides — capital goods and consumption goods — economic growth appears as a
self-perpetuating process.

   If the expansion of the market represents the general condition
of technical change, the increase of real wages[1][see SYLOS-LABINI
(1984)] and the growth of investment [see STEINDL(1974)] represent
two other relevant factors.

   On the one hand, increases in productivity are both cause and
effect of the long-run increase in money wages relative to prices. As
cause, the increase in productivity induces workers to demand higher
wages.[2] As effect, firms may offset wage increases by saving labour,

---

[1] According to Sylos-Labini, we should distinguish between the two ratios $\frac{C_L}{P}$ and
$\frac{W}{P_{MA}}$ (where C_L = labour cost per unit of output, and P_{MA} = price of machinery), in
order to analyse separately the immediate and delayed effects of changes in money
wages relative to prices.

[2] When productivity increases, firms themselves may decide without any pressure

either increasing the subdivision of labour or introducing machines. If we distinguish between industrial prices in general and the prices of machines, in the case of wages outpacing the prices of machines firms will find it more profitable to save labour by substituting machines for workers.

On the other hand, investment is a source of productivity growth in so far as innovations are embodied in new plant and machinery. This implies the consideration of the determinants of the level of investment, within the analysis of the process of 'division of labour–technical change'; if this should be primarily demand pressure, as expressed by the degree of utilized capacity and current profits as the source of self-financing, then in this case too the variables are mutually related. Investment stimulates the process of innovation and increases productivity and, in its turn, an increase in productivity brings an increase of profits and then influences the level of investment.[3]

2) As is well known, it has been traditional to divide the analysis of technical change into three branches: invention, the creation of new products and processes; innovation, the transfer of invention to commercial application; and diffusion, the spread of innovation into the economic environment. Unfortunately, as some authors have already noted, this has provided a somewhat fragmented approach to the study of technical change in which interdependence and feedback between the stages have been lost. The classical concept of technical change does not present this inconvenience, owing to the different levels of analysis on which is based: 1) a 'macro'level, which considers the effects of the division of labour on the whole economic system and 2) a 'micro' level, which concentrates on any individual working process.[4]

---

to grant higher wages to attract — and to keep — the most efficient workers and to ensure a peaceable atmosphere within the firm. See in Ch.2, Babbage's 'New system of manufacturing'; also Mill's discussion of co-operation between capitalists and workers.

[3] There is an additional factor that may be considered: the expected rate of profits. According to KALECKI(1954),the influence of technical progress on investment results from the expectation of additional profits for the innovator, who introduces a new product or a new process. Also in this case, there is a positive feedback. In both cases there is a time lag involved. See also KALECKI(1940).

[4] This dual point of view is, first of all, motivated by the different nature of the

As a result, the classical framework permits one both to study the impact of technical change on the process of economic growth (macro perspective) and to explore the determinants of the innovative process, at firm level (micro perspective). In this light the distinction between invention, innovation and diffusion, whilst conceptually valid of course, loses importance: they all become different stages in the evolution of technology which is dominated by accumulation and learning.

3.3   Division of labour and increasing returns

Having said that division of labour and technical change are both intimately related to increasing returns, we must now deal with static and dynamic[5] definitions of increasing returns and the respective concepts of economic progress.

To do this, let us start by assuming that the process of production may be described as a sequence of m elementary operations that can be performed by men and/or machines. Moreover, let us suppose that a certain job, such as the production of a ware, is to be performed on a certain scale (q) and that for producing the quantity q, k workers are necessary.[6]

In the absence of division of labour (pre-capitalistic situation), each of the workers will perform all the job — being more or less

---

processes of division of labour. Whereas the social division of labour bases itself on the complementary nature of roles and on the necessary adjustment of the economic structure to the needs of the society, the industrial division of labour is directed to optimize each process of production. Secondly, but not of secondary importance, it reflects the various motivations (philosophical, political, mathematical,etc.) that are behind the classical analysis of the division of labour.

[5]In our terms, a *static* model is one that embodies a series of logical possibilities, independent of time. On the contrary, a dynamic model isolates certain groups of phenomena in order to explain their relations and their behaviour in the course of time; therefore a *dynamic* model is one in which variables must be *irreversibly* dated.

[6]It is worth noticing that each operation is not necessarily associated with one person. There might be cases in which a single elementary operation has to be performed, for example, by 10 workers. For this reason k will be usually greater or equal to m. In any case we assume that on replicating an operation, the number of workers performing it automatically doubles.

aware of the sequence of elementary operations which are performed
— at his own pace and with his own skill.[7]

But once the division of labour is adopted, all elementary operations are detected, each worker specializes in performing only one
operation and this brings increases of productivity [for the reasons
illustrated by the classical economists and discussed in Ch. 2]. Let
us consider as an example a process of production with $k = m = 3$;
it can be represented as follows:

$$
\begin{array}{llll}
a1 & b2 & c3 & \\
 & a1 & b2 & c3 \\
 & & a1 & b2 & c3 \\
 & & & a1 & b2 & c3 \\
 & & & & etc & \cdots \\
\end{array}
$$

time →

where worker a performs only operation 1, worker b only operation 2
and worker c only operation 3. Each individual, in this regime, must
work at a certain pace defined by a co-ordinator. Owing to the supervision, it is possible to adapt individual powers to the operations to
be performed and to create opportunities for mechanizing some stage
of the process [Babbage's *principle of economy of skill*].

Now, the question is: what sort of economies of scale does the
division of labour generate? Before answering this question we must
clarify what we mean by 'scale'.

Here the concept of scale refers not so much to the total output
of a firm, but, in particular, to the output of a line of production.
It could therefore be defined, following GOLD(1981), as the level of

---

[7]We consider skill as the dexterity of a worker in performing the job, owing
to learning and training.In our view, the specialization of tasks caused by the division of labour does not necessarily reduce the skill of the workers: every time
increased specialization is accompanied by a process of learning it brings an increase of skill.The experience of the Western countries suggests that the importance of training rises as industrialization advances. In particular, 'maintenance'
workers (who are typically highly trained) increase in importance relative to production workers. Moreover, professional and technical personnel grow rapidly in
their relative importance, as do clerical and kindred personnel [see MOMIGLIANO-
SINISCALCO(1982), STANBACK(1981)].

planned production capacity (of a line of production) which determines the extent to which division of labour has been applied to a
unified operation.[8] This definition has two main advantages:
  (i) by emphasizing the planned structure of a unified production
process, this definition takes account of the fact that the division of
labour is the organizing principle of production and not just the result
of natural or innate differences between individuals;
  (ii) it offers an operational basis for differentiating 'scale' from
'size' — where size is, of course, equal to the scale multiplied by the
number of lines of production.
  To distinguish between scale and size is important for two reasons: 1) whereas an increase in size implies the risk of increasing
concentration or the emergence of monopoly power, increases in scale
do not necessarily have these implications [see Ch.6 for a more detailed discussion of such a topic]; 2) such a distinction allows one to
recognize that mere increases in size [involving duplication of smaller
scale relationships, or the intermittent accretion of diverse production
units] may yield no production economies at all. As CLARK(1923)
has noted 'if the plant grows piecemeal without having been carefully
planned to make such growth possible, the result may be an increase
rather than a decrease in costs"(p.104).[9]

Economies of scale   Going back to our question, we can now say that,
according to the classical viewpoint, the advantages of scale do not
derive automatically from sheer size, but reside in the potential for

---

[8]This definition is obviously in contrast with the traditional static one which
defines increases in scale as involving increases in the size or capacity of production
units, provided that there are no changes in factor proportions — or, by direct
implication, in the products made and in the basic technologies employed. Thus
the final outcome is essentially an enlarged duplicate of the smaller scale unit. For an
in-depth discussion of the limits of the traditional concept of scale, see GOLD(1981).
  [9]On this point Clark's *Economics of Overhead Costs* (1923) is particularly illuminating. His discussion of 'How and Why Large Plants Bring Economy' directs
attention to the important role of technological change in supporting increases in the
size of factories through the development of another dimension of specialization —
research and other forms of improved knowledge — which engenders continuing improvements in products, processes, facilities and managerial capabilities. Although
Clark focuses on size alone, his awareness of the need for some qualification of the
size criterion is apparent in the warning quoted in the main text.

task specialization and improved work organization, in the possibility of using and inventing specialized production equipment, in the acquisition of skill in the manufacturing process.

In both its forms — subdivision and displacement of labour — the intra-firm division of labour generates two main kinds of internal economies: 1) *longer-series* and 2) *parallel-series* scale economies.[10]

1) As 'the extent of the market' grows, opportunities arise for further efficient subdivision of the productive process into a greater number of elementary operations. Moreover, the consequent simplification of tasks may allow machines to perform them, and mechanization, in turn renews the sources of economies of scale. Referring to the example, suppose that each stage of what was previously a three-stage line of production is subdivided into two. Suppose further that it is then discovered that a certain operation can be mechanized. At the old scale of production the new machine may be idle 90% of the time. In this case, the most economical scale of production has multiplied tenfold.

2) Suppose that one of the workers (e.g. worker b) employed in the line of production is idle half the time. Then double the output can be had simply by doubling his utilization rate and the production can be organized as follows:

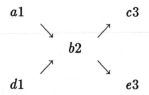

where $d1$ and $e3$ are replications of, respectively, $a1$ and $c3$, with reference to a single line of production.

When a machine, instead of a worker, is idle for half the time it cannot, of course, be replaced by half machine employed all the time; but it may be possible to double its utilization if it can be shared between two parallel lines of production (provided that the firm expects to be able to sell twice the output). These parallel-series

---

[10]We borrow these denominations from LEIJONHUFVUD(1986), pp.213-4.

economies are probably never totally exhausted; however it is clear that, if we keep the number of serial stages constant, these economies of parallel replication become less and less significant as output is increased. Thus, they depend on the division of labour so far as this increases the number of elementary operations to be performed within the productive process [cf. GEORGESCU–ROEGEN(1972)].

In brief, both kinds of internal economies of scale generated by the intra-firm division of labour manifest themselves by an increase in the number of operations which compose the process of production, either in the form of new stages of production or as replications of operations already performed.[11]

In both cases the process of 'division of labour–technical change' presents two essential features:

1. the *ordering* — it proceeds by a succession of steps (subsequent increases in the number of operations performed within the productive process), each of which represents a certain increase of productivity due to organizational and/or technical innovation;

2. the *element of time* — which elapses between one step and the following one and which must be regarded as a random variable, because of the unpredictability of changes.

There is also a third factor to be considered: *accumulation of knowledge*. Extensions of scale beyond the frontiers of current experience patently require searching for additional technological knowledge by considering the possibilities of modifying past practices and evaluating their prospective effects. These may involve altering material specifications, equipment characteristics, input proportions, operating speeds and conditions, labour tasks, maintenance requirements, etc..

---

[11]*N.B.*: There is indeed a third kind of economies which are generated by duplicating the existing arrangements once the optimal combination of factors is reached (Babbage's principle of numerical proportions). Given our definition of scale, this kind of economies would be better denominated as 'economies of size'. In this context we ignore them, but they will be considered in Ch.6, when we analyse the implications of the division of labour in terms of theory of the firm and market forms.

These processes are not unidirectional. Improvements in technology also tend to alter the potentials of specialization and, hence, the prospective benefits of further increases in scale. Moreover such interactions tend to be reasonably continuous because innovations in technology within any subsection of the production process tend to engender accomodating adjustments in antecedent and subsequent subsections in a kind of ripple-effect — as a result of the unceasing pressure to optimize the effective organization of operations as a whole.

These three characteristics of the process of 'division of labour-technical change' are at the basis of the formal analysis which we will carry out in the second part of the book. In the following chapter we will introduce two stochastic models which aim to describe the dynamic economies of scale generated by both subdivision of labour and displacement of labour within a single process of production. In Ch.5, we will bring our analysis to a macro level, highlighting the link existing between the division of labour, considered as a stochastic process, on the one hand, and the progress functions, on the other hand; hence, concentrating attention on the key elements that influence the economy's productivity performance.

In the meantime, we can synthesize the dynamic nature of the economies of scale generated by the process of 'division of labour-technical change' in defining productivity not as a function of current output (as in the case of static economies of scale), but as a function of cumulative output, i.e. the sum of output flows in the past $[N_t = \sum_t q_t$, in discrete time, $= \int_0^t q_t \, dt$, in continuous time]. Cumulative output stands for the element of time in a twofold manner: 1) given that changes are discontinuous and unpredictable, time is depicted as *event time*, i.e. in accordance with the pace of the innovation process; 2) to take account of the accumulation of knowledge due to the process of improvement by practice, time is also memory of the past.

In FIG.3.1 we indicate on the x-axis the cumulative output (N_t) and on the y-axis labour productivity (π). In accordance with the above considerations, the growth of productivity under dynamic increasing returns may be represented by a step function: each time an

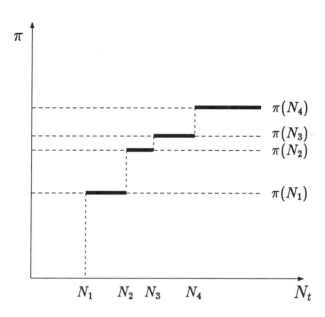

Figure 3.1: **Productivity growth under dynamic increasing returns**

innovation (organizational, technological, etc..) is introduced, productivity jumps up. In the time gap between two innovations productivity keeps constant, as shown by the dotted horizontal straight lines, each corresponding to a specific structure of technology and, therefore, depending by a specific value of N_t. Each change in productivity is irreversible, given that it corresponds to a change of scale and scaling a process of production up or down does change the physical processes within it, the relationships between its parts and its connections to the rest of the production system, the number of people involved, their tasks, their skills and their relationship with one another.

The classical postulates   The next question is: does the process of increasing returns ever reach a ceiling? In other words, are the economies of scale generated by the process of 'division of labour–

technical change' never ending? It is not easy to answer this question. What we can say is that most classical economists had an unswerving trust in the process of technical change and the ability of division of labour and mechanization to propel society to ever higher levels of prosperity. However, they did not ignore the existence of boundary conditions which might bring the economic system to a stationary state. Existing professions and trades, prevailing technologies, 'vexacious institutions', public mismanagement are all examples of possible limits to growth.

In brief, the forces commanding the process of increasing returns generated by the division of labour are captured by two basic 'postulates':

1. productivity is an increasing function of the division of labour;

2. the division of labour is limited by the extent of the market.

Since per capita income is basically dependent upon productivity, income becomes a function of the division of labour and the extent of the market, and income growth, i.e. economic development, thus becomes a process of expanding markets and dividing labour. The thrust of this argument is illustrated by the curves in FIG.3.2 and 3.3.

The curves in FIG.3.2 translate the classical postulates in terms of long-run cost curves (quadrant IV) and short-run supply curves (quadrant I). The short-run supply curves in quadrant I are parallel to the x-axis due to the time gap between the introduction of two subsequent innovations. Given the discontinuity of technological changes, costs and supplies change suddenly in correspondence to specific value of N_t.

The process of 'division of labour–technical change' generates a long-run tendency to falling prices as a result of the self-propelling process of structural change (quadrant IV). As we stressed above, division of labour yields not only the static advantages of specialization, but also dynamic advantages through learning-by-experience and technological improvements. This feature of the process is represented by the relationship between average costs and cumulative output. More cumulative output grows through time less costly the

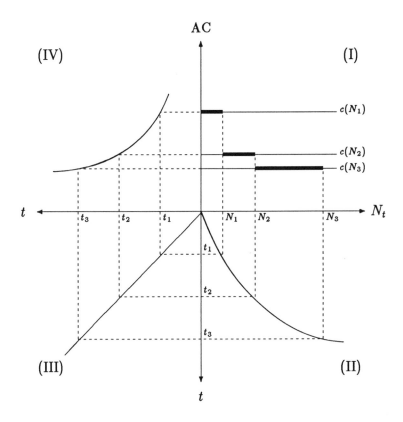

Figure 3.2: **A graphical representation of the classical 'postulates'**

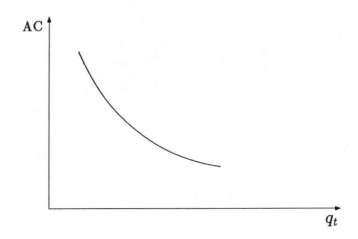

Figure 3.3: **Average costs under dynamic increasing returns**

production of current output becomes, being N_t a proxy for experience gained by successive production improvements. The history of production comes therefore to influence the path which costs take.[12]

Considering directly the relation between average costs and current output, the classical postulates imply the existence of a downward sloping average costs curve[13] [see FIG.3.3]. This is consistent with Sraffa's (1926) argument that:

---

[12]*N.B.*: It would be interesting to study what path N_t should follow so as to obtain increasing or U-shaped cost curves. In this perspective, one might be keen to re-examine Sraffa's 1925 criticism of Marshallian U-shaped cost curves. See, on this topic, TALAMO(1976).

[13]At the level of the individual firm we might imagine that the average costs fall until the limit of the plant's capacity is reached:

> Everyday experience shows that a very large number of
> undertakings and the majority of those which produce
> manufactured consumer goods work under conditions of
> individual diminishing costs. (...) Businessmen, who re-
> gard themselves as being subject to competitive condi-
> tions, would consider absurd the assertion that the limit
> to their production is to be found in the internal condi-
> tions of production in their firms, which do not permit
> the production of a greater quantity without an increase
> in costs (p.543).

It is also consistent with a great deal of empirical evidence [see SYLOS-LABINI(1982)].

However, the above considerations do not allow us to give a clear-cut answer to the above question. It seems therefore appropriate to say that the classical division-of-labour theory leaves open whether productivity increases without limit or increases forever asymptotically to an upper limit.[It is beyond the aims of this work to develop further research in this direction.]

Meanwhile, the relationship between the division of labour and the extent of the market may be seen as determining the growth path of the economy: on the one hand, output growth causes — through an increasing division of labour — a reduction of labour input, i.e. growth of productivity; on the other hand, productivity growth results in a fall of prices relative to wages and thereby stimulates both demand and output.

However, for individual industries growth is not always unidirectional. At some point, industrial demand may reach a peak, and then begin to decline as substitutes are invented and economic growth shifts to other locations. Because much of the movement is irreversible, the decline of an industry would not take place on the path along which it expanded, however, but rather along a higher, flatter path like that shown in FIG.3.4.

Division of labour

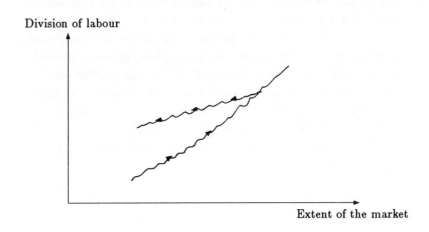

Extent of the market

Figure 3.4: **The division of labour and the extent of the
market: expansion and contraction paths**

3.4 Dynamic increasing returns and equilibrium theory

Modern equilibrium analysis found it difficult to come to grips with
the dynamic features of the division of labour, and it is presumably
at least partly for this reason that the division of labour was dropped
as an important subject from the economic textbooks.[14]

It is difficult to identify any exact borderline between the classical approach and the modern one. However, it must be stressed
that Alfred Marshall was the first economist to consider the association between division of labour and increasing returns, in the light
of equilibrium theory. Indeed, he devoted no less than three chapters of his *Principles of Economics* (1890, Book IV, Chs.9-11) to the
division of labour, not only covering most of the points traditionally

---

[14]Attempts to remove division of labour from economics were also based on other
grounds. Some economists felt such discussion to be more appropriate to technical books of production engineering and factor management [see ROBBINS(1932),
pp.32-8]; others wished to confine analysis of its effects to sociological studies as-
sessing the general impact of division of labour on society.

dealt with by the classical economists, but often introducing subtle modifications. The main modifications which we are concerned with are, on one side, the consideration of the division of labour as a simple mechanism of static adjustment to the environment at firm level, and, on the other side, the definition of increasing returns as a reversible relation between factors of production and output, at the industry level.

In what follows we will try to show how harmful these modifications may be for the theory of division of labour.

3.4.1 Marshall's treatment of the division of labour

In his *Principles*, Marshall sought (but failed) to consider the economic system as an organic whole subject to biological laws. The firm, which can be considered the elementary unit of the system, is subject to a life cycle (birth, growth and death) which is ruled by two factors: 1)the adjustment of the firm to the environment and 2) the state of entrepreneurial faculties.

The division of labour — considered only as intra-firm division of labour — is connected with both these factors:

1. it is willed by the entrepreneur who makes up his mind on the basis of the *actual extent* of the market (i.e. current output) and the demand for the particular commodity he/she produces;

2. it is a means of adjustment to the environment, since it is the cause of internal economies[15] which allow the firms to improve their efficiency (i.e. to survive in their struggle for existence).[16]

---

[15]Marshall calls external economies, those dependent on the general development of the industry; whereas, he calls internal economies, 'those dependent on the resources of the individual houses of business (..),on their organization and the efficiency of their management'(p.266).

[16]According to Marshall:

the development of the organisms, whether social or physical, involves an increasing subdivision of functions between its separate parts on the one hand, and on the other a more intimate connection with them. (..)This increased subdivision of functions, or 'differentiation', as is called, manifests itself with regard to industry in such forms as the

The introduction of machinery is part of this adjustment to the environment, but only by cheapening and making more accurate the work which has been already reduced to routine.[17]

It is important to note the differences between this concept of division of labour and the classical one. Far from being a simple change of emphasis, Marshall's definition of division of labour implicitly neglects the flow of innovations introduced by the rationalization of the process of production, the propelling role of the market and the interrelationship between firm and industry levels of analysis.

Moreover, being aware of the problem of expressing competitive equilibrium conditions in the presence of internal economies generated by the division of labour (cf.p.459,n.1) Marshall considers external[18] economies as the only cause of decreasing cost of production. Given the link 'division of labour-firm level-internal economies of scale' established by Marshall, this choice obviously plays down the division of labour.

---

division of labour, and the development of specialized skill, knowledge and machinery; while 'integration', that is, a growing intimacy and firmness of the connections between the separate parts of the industrial organism, shows itself in such forms as the increase of security of commercial credit, and of the means and habits of communications by sea and road, by railway and telegraph, by post and printing-press (p.241).

[17]In Marshall's words:'any manufacturing operation that can be reduced to uniformity, so that exactly the same thing has to be done over and over again in the same way, is sure to be taken over sooner or later by machinery'; 'the chief effect of the improvement of machinery is to cheapen and make more accurate the work which would anyhow have been subdivided'(p.255).

[18]To apply the categories 'internal' and 'external' to the dynamic economies of scale generated by the process of 'division of labour–technical change' is indeed difficult. It is very often the case that variations in the condition of production of one firm will act not merely upon its own costs, but also upon the costs of other firms, not only within the same industry. As SRAFFA(1926) stresses, under increasing returns, reductions in cost which are due to external economies — to which Marshall refers — are incompatible with the conditions of partial equilibrium analysis; in fact the class of economies most commonly met is that of those which are external from the viewpoint of the individual firm, but not internal as regards the industry in its aggregate: 'in such a case the conditions of the 'particular equilibrium' which it was intended to isolate are upset, and it is no longer possible, without contradiction to neglect collateral effects'[SRAFFA(1926), p.539].

Marshall looks for the sources of increasing returns to scale in such phenomena as are permitted by a static framework, including redeployments and adaptations of factors (especially labour) as well as *minor* improvements. Structural changes in factors or products are completely excluded:

> we exclude from view any economies that may result from substantive new inventions; but we include those which may be expected to arise naturally out of adaptations of existing ideas; and we look towards a position of balance or equilibrium between the forces of progress and decay, which would be attained if the conditions under view were supposed to act uniformly for a long time (p.460).

In Marshall's attempt to conciliate increasing returns with the partial equilibrium analysis, the distinction between firm and industry levels of analysis becomes particularly relevant. This is true for at least two reasons: 1) according to Marshall, 'increasing returns' has a different meaning, according to whether we refer to the whole industry or to the single firm [19]; 2) determining the normal equilibrium, in Marshall's statical method, implies the assumption of 'ceteris paribus', which, given Marshall's concepts, is more adaptable to the industry level of analysis. Problems of adjustment of the individual firm through time[20], and the inevitable 'decay of entrepreneurial faculties' (implicit in the life cycle analogy) make the rise and fall of individual firms frequent,'while a great industry is going through one long oscillation, or even moving steadily forwards'(p.457).[21]

---

[19]In Marshall's words: 'The tendency to a fall in the price of a commodity as a result of a gradual development of the industry by which it is made, is quite a different thing from the tendency to the rapid introduction of new economies by an individual firm that is increasing its business'(p.457). Moreover, 'the causes which govern the facilities for production at the command of a single firm, (..)conform to quite different laws from those which control the whole output of an industry'(p.457).

[20]Difficulties of expanding their own special markets with the consequent slowness or inability to exploit potential economies of scale; technical and organizational problems related to 'the length of time that is necessarily occupied by each individual business in extending its internal and still more its external organization'(p.500). These factors play an important role in Marshall's exercise of reconciling static increasing returns with some sort of 'competitive' regime.

[21]Marshall's way out of Cournot's dilemma is very 'simple': he states, using a

3.4.2   The Appendix H

In Marshall's 'biological model', every process of structural change needs such a long time that it is almost impossible to analyse its whole result. For this reason, Marshall goes step by step, breaking up any complex question and studying one bit at a time; in breaking it up he can also isolate some tendencies by the assumption 'ceteris paribus' and in this way their 'disturbing effects' can be neglected for a time.

This arrangement of the difficulties arising from the 'element of time', leads Marshall to adopt a *static* method and to move the analysis to the *industry level*, drawing on the *representative firm*.[22] Given the size of the industry (in terms of level of output), the representative firm has two main properties: 1)its output remains constant (if and only if industry output remains constant); 2)its cost per unit of output is representative of the industry at that level of production. On the basis of these two characteristics, Marshall draws the supply curve for the industry as the locus of points representing the expenses of production of the representative firm for different given levels of output [cf. MARSHALL(1920), p.344]. Then, crossing demand and supply curves, Marshall determines the 'normal' prices of the commodities, namely those 'average' values, which 'the economic forces would bring about if the general conditions of life were stationary for a run of time long enough to enable them all to work out their full effect'(p.347).

In the long-run the size of the representative firm, by definition, is governed, other things being equal, by the general expansion of the industry. Therefore, a gradual increase in demand increases gradually

---

biological analogy, that equilibrium of total output does not in fact require that all firms be in equilibrium. Industry output can be constant through time, even though some firms are being born and growing, and others declining and dying, provided that the gains in output from the one cause are balanced by the losses in output from the other.

[22]Such a firm is purely a mental construct and it is not pretended that it is likely to have a real existence, although Marshall occasionally argued that way. It is 'simply' a method of depicting *industrial* equilibrium in terms of the theory of the firm. On this interpretation of the representative firm see KALDOR(1934) and ROBBINS(1928).

its size and its efficiency. 'That is to say, when making lists of supply prices (supply schedules) for long periods in these industries, we
set down a diminished supply price against an increased amount of
the flow of the goods; meaning thereby that a flow of that increased
amount will in the course of time be supplied profitably at that lower
price, to meet a fairly steady corresponding demand'(p.460).

This is the reason why Marshall refers to the representative firm in
order to draw the long-period 'normal'supply curve for a commodity
which obeys the law of increasing returns (downward sloping) [see
FIG.3.5(a) : p= *expenses of production of the representative firm*; q=
scale of production ='*normal*' *output*].[23]

This curve, according to Marshall, is really located in three dimensions, representing scale of production, expenses of production
and preparation-time[24] respectively:

> We could get much nearer to nature if we allowed our-
> selves a more complex illustration. We might take a series
> of curves, of which the first allowed for the economies likely
> to be introduced as the result of each increase in the scale
> of production during one year, a second curve doing the
> same for two years, a third for three years, and so on. Cut-
> ting them out of cardboard and standing them up side by
> side, we should obtain a surface, of which the three dimen-

[23]Let us consider Marshall's way of drawing the supply curve for the industry, adding up the individual supply curves of the firms which compose it. As
SRAFFA(1925) has stressed, it is impossible to add-up curves which shift because
of their dependence on internal and external economies. This is why Marshall ends
up by making the equilibrium of the firm depend upon the equilibrium of the industry rather than the other way round. Eliminating the effect of the intra-firm
division of labour from the analysis, he can first postulate the conditions of equilibrium for the industry (considering only the external economies) and then create
an analytical device — the representative firm — which answers the requirements
of the statical equilibrium scheme.

[24]By preparation time is meant the time necessary for introducing the economies
which an expansion of the scale makes possible.'One difficulty arises from the fact
that a suitable time to allow for the introduction of the economies appertaining to
one increase in the scale of production is not long enough for another and larger
increase, so we must fix on some fairly long time ahead, which is likely to be indicated by the special problem in hand, and adjust the whole series of supply prices
to it.'(p.809,n.2).

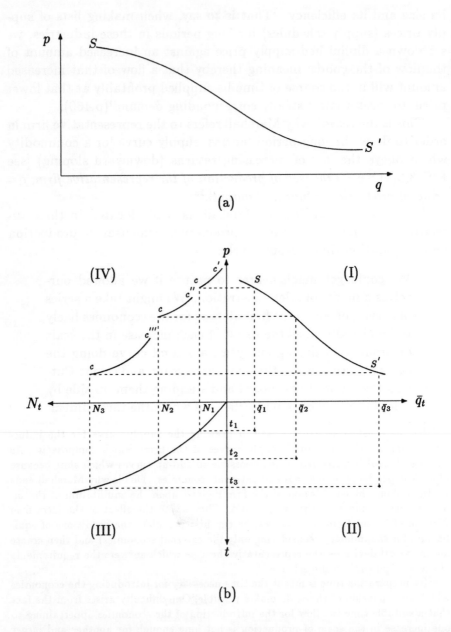

(a)

(b)

Figure 3.5: **Marshall's 'normal' supply curve under increasing returns**

sions represented amount, price, and time respectively. If we had marked on each curve the point corresponding to that amount which, so far as can be foreseen, seems likely to be the normal amount for the year to which that curve related, then these points would form a curve on the surface, and that curve would be a fairly true long-period normal supply curve for a commodity obeying the law of increasing returns (p.809,n.2).

Let us show the limits of this curve referring to FIG.3.5(b). In the four quadrants we have respectively: i)the long-run supply curve; ii)the expected 'normal' output of the year $(\bar{q}_t)$; iii)cumulative output (growing through time) as a measure of preparation time; iv)cost curves allowing for the economies of scale likely to be introduced as the result of each increase in the scale of production during a certain number of years (CC' = one year, CC" = two years, etc..). Curve SS' is drawn through time: for each year it is possible to define the expenses of production of the representative firm corresponding to a certain expected level of 'normal' output, bearing in mind that costs diminish due to external economies of scale [given that the representative firm represents the industry it does not have any sense to speak of internal economies, by definition].

Indeed, because of the way in which this curve is drawn, it seems to stand for a history of the successive attainment of various scales of production, rather than a range of alternatively choosable, mutually exclusive positions [cf. SHACKLE(1972)]. Thus, if the purpose of confronting with each other a demand curve and a supply curve is to exhibit the mode of determination of that price-quantity pair which can represent both demand conditions and supply conditions simultaneously, Marshall's long-period supply curve *cannot* serve this purpose, since it must call upon a forecast of demand conditions in order that its own shape may be known [see quadrant II in FIG.3.5(b)].

Nevertheless, Marshall uses this curve to determine stable equilibrium between demand and supply [see FIG.3.6].

Implicit in this scheme of equilibrium, we find a concept of *static reversible increasing returns*, since Marshall assumes that 'if the

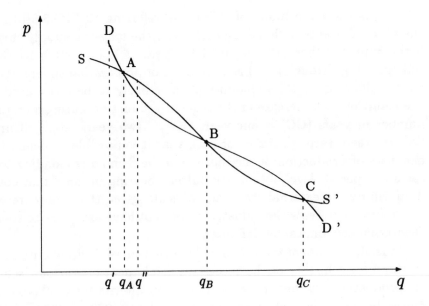

Figure 3.6: **Equilibrium of demand and supply under static increasing returns**

normal production of a commodity increases and afterwards again diminishes to its old amount, the demand price and the supply price will return to their old position for that amount'(p.807-8). This assumption is necessary for the existence of two or more positions of stable equilibrium of demand and supply. Let us consider, for example, the point of stable equilibrium A, in FIG.3.6. The long-period supply price might be either greater or less than the normal demand price for the corresponding scale of production. In the latter case (q') 'undertakers, looking forward to the life of a firm started in that trade, considering its chances of prosperity and decay, discounting its future outlays and its future incomings, would conclude that the latter showed a good balance over the former. Capital and Labour would stream rapidly into the trade'(p.806). On the contrary, in the former case (q''), capital and labour would avoid the trade.

Marshall is aware that 'this theory is out of touch with real conditions of life', in so far as it ignores that 'when any casual disturbance has caused a great increase in the production of any commodity, and thereby has led to the introduction of extensive economies, these economies are not readily lost.'(pp.807-8). However, most equilibrium theory has been built up on these concepts according to Marshall's belief that the 'statical treatment alone can give us definiteness and precision of thoughts'(p.461).

3.5 Conclusions

Briefly, in this chapter we have dealt with three matters: 1)the analysis of the link between division of labour and technical change; 2)the description of the process of dynamic increasing returns generated by the division of labour; 3)the comparison between the classical approach to economic change and the one based on equilibrium theory.

We have shown that whereas equilibrium theory focuses on statical increasing returns and assumes that the conditions of production and the demand for a commodity can be considered, in respect to small variations, as being practically independent, both in regard to each other and in relation to the supply and demand of all other commodities, in a classical perspective, economic progress consists of a cumulative and self-perpetuating process of change. The economy must be viewed as an interrelated whole in a state of constant and internally generated change.

Although it appears difficult to define any exact borderline between the classical approach and the modern one, we have argued that Marshall's theory of economic change has some harmful implications for the division-of-labour theory:

- it confines the division of labour to the firm level and does not stress positively the importance of the flow of innovations which the industrial division of labour generates;

- it plays down the division of labour by concentrating the analysis at the industry level through the device of the representative firm.

- it represents the process of increasing returns as a reversible relationship.

On the contrary, in our view, division of labour and technical change are both intimately related to dynamic — therefore, irreversible — increasing returns. Economies of scale (where scale stands for the planned production capacity of a line of production) are generated by the progressive task specialization and improved work organization, and by the possibility of using and inventing specialized production equipment. They do not derive automatically from sheer size, but from the potential for improvements in organization and technology which size brings.

An understanding of the mechanism of increasing returns requires, in our view, analysis at two different levels: of the capacity of firms to generate a particular technological performance; and of the interaction between firms within a market environment in which their technological differences are resolved into changes of quantities and prices. In the study of the process of division of labour–technical change we have found it useful to develop these two analyses separately. In Ch.4 we concentrate on the stochastic process which determines a certain revealed technological performance of the firm. In Ch.5 we consider dynamic increasing returns in a production model based on the interrelation among industries.

PART II
FORMAL REPRESENTATIONS OF THE PROCESS OF DIVISION OF LABOUR

4 Stochastic models of division of labour

4.1 Introduction

In the previous chapters we have stressed the relevance of the relationship between division of labour and technical change for the purpose of our research. Taking as our point of reference the works of certain classical authors, we have introduced the concept of dynamic increasing returns to scale and suggested the advantages of adopting the classical conceptualization of technical change.

Now, in this chapter, we deal with some of the methodological problems implicit in our approach. In particular, we concentrate our attention on the possibility of drawing on stochastic analysis to formalize the process of 'division of labour–technical change'.

As in other steps of our work, we have, first of all, looked at the existing literature in order to identify possible useful contributions along the same line of research. The results of this investigation are summarized in the first part of this chapter.

Secondly, we have tried to specify our theoretical framework in a dynamic model suitable for dealing with the economies of scale generated by the process of 'division of labour–technical change'. In the following pages, we describe the random character of the various forms of industrial division of labour and we introduce two stochastic models of intra-firm division of labour. The choice of the firm-level is mainly

dictated by the interest of focusing on 'internal' economies of scale —
usually neglected within the economic analysis of technical change.
In the next chapter the analysis will be enlarged to consider all sorts
of economies which characterize the process of dynamic increasing
returns.

It must be stressed very clearly that this work does not aspire to
make a contribution to the mathematics of stochastic processes. We
approach this mathematics as an economist interested in describing
the behaviour of aggregates that is hard to approximate by a deterministic model. We are aware that, from a mathematical point of
view, our analysis is 'naive' in so far as it makes use of concepts and
methods that would need more rigorous treatment. However, in doing so, we hope to be able to carry out an adequate analysis with a
minimum of mathematical machinery and to make it intelligible to
others besides professional mathematicians.

4.2   Stochastic processes in economics

Random elements may be introduced into a formal apparatus in two
ways. First, by a difference (or any functional) equation containing
a term with a random variable. [This random term usually enters
the equation as an additive disturbance, and it plays the role of an
exogenous factor].

Alternatively, functional equations are set up for the distribution
function of the random variables.In a dynamic context, this means
to refer to stochastic processes. In mathematical terms a stochastic
process can be defined as an arbitrary family of random variables X_t,
where t is a parameter running over a suitable index set T (that can
be either continuous or discrete). A stochastic process moves from
one state to the next as time goes on and each transition is, or may
be in principle, influenced by chance; but it is no less influenced by
bias, that is, by systematic influences.

Economists have drawn on stochastic processes, at first, in order to explain how stable economic distributions — that appear in a
wide range of empirical data — can be created by random processes.
From the pioneering work of GIBRAT(1930), KALECKI(1945) and

SIMON(1955)[1] stochastic theories of the size distribution of firms have tried to explain observed size differences among firms as a consequence of random growth rate differences, accumulated over time. More recently this kind of analysis has turned to investigate more directly the causal linkage between the level of concentration and the pace and pattern of innovation [NELSON–WINTER(1982)].[2] Moreover, great attention has been devoted to technology diffusion [HORNER(1977)], especially under increasing returns [ARTHUR(1983),(1987),(1988)].

4.2.1 Some pioneering works

Let us concentrate on the pioneering works summarized in TAB.4.1. The common idea underlying those works is that certain economic distributions are stable — to a point at least, though not altogether. In particular, Gibrat found that many economic distributions conform approximately to normality, if the variables in question are transformed to logarithms. To explain the emergence of this regular pattern, he proposed a 'law of proportionate effect' (better known as 'Gibrat's law'), which says that in a process of growth, *equal proportionate increments have the same chance of occurring in a given time-interval whatever size happens to have been reached.* In so doing, he considers a special kind of stochastic process called *random walk.* In the most elementary kind of random walk we consider discrete equal time-intervals, and an object which wanders on an infinite straight line, taking, in each time-interval, a step either in one or the other direction, with probability p and q respectively $(p + q = 1)$. The random walk considered by Gibrat is, in fact, more complicated, since the steps taken at each time-interval are themselves random variables, independent of each other and identically distributed. It has been shown that, in virtue of this, the variance of the distribution increases in proportion to time and that, as $t \to \infty$, it becomes infinite (tendency to diffusion).

---

[1]A similar stochastic approach has been applied to the analysis of income distribution in CHAMPERNOWNE(1953). Other important contributions are in HART–PRAIS(1956), ADELMAN(1958) and STEINDL(1965).

[2]In a different perspective, changes in technology as a creative process of generation of new skills are discussed in AMENDOLA–GAFFARD(1988).

	Random process	Stationary solution
GIBRAT KALECKI	Random walk (discrete time)	Log–normal distribution : $f(i) = \dfrac{1}{\sqrt{2\pi}\sigma} e^{-\frac{1}{2}[\frac{log i - \mu}{\sigma}]^2}$
SIMON	Birth-and-death (continuous time)	Yule distribution: $f(i) = A\,B(i, \rho + 1) =$ $= A\,\dfrac{\Gamma(i)\,\Gamma(\rho + 1)}{\Gamma(i + \rho + 1)}$

Table 4.1: **Pioneering works in stochastic models of economic processes**

Many modifications of the law of proportionate effect have been proposed, aiming to offset the tendency to diffusion, characteristic of the 'unrestricted' random walk adopted by Gibrat.

Both Kalecki and Simon have introduced stability conditions to 'impede' the random growth. On the one hand, Kalecki has assumed that the proportionate random increment is negatively correlated with the size. It has been shown that under this restriction the variance of a sample of identical firms remains constant in spite of the process of random growth.

On the other hand, Simon has assumed that the unrestricted random walk does apply to a sample of identical firms, but that there is a stream of small new firms entering, and of old firms dying, which offsets the increase in variance for the firms as a whole. In this model changes can take place at random points of (continuous) time, not at certain intervals only. This possibility leads in the simplest case to a Poisson process, and in slightly more complicated cases to a birth-and-death process. Simon's model is an example of the latter; accordingly, the 'law of proportionate effect' is replaced by the 'population law' which says that *the number of births is in proportion to the size of the population.* Under such condition, there is no correlation between growth rate and size, and, as Simon shows, the stationary solution for the birth-and-death process is a Yule distribution.

Notwithstanding the differences among the above models, they all present two main characteristics: they refer to *homogeneous, ergodic* Markov processes.[3] On the one hand, homogeneous Markov processes are usually adopted because, working with stationary probabilities, the mathematics becomes much more tractable. On the other hand,ergodicity implies the existence of a stationary distribution over the various states of the process. The frequency with which the process occupies a possible state tends to this stationary distribution. As a result, knowing the exact starting conditions of the process (or an exact description at any point in time) becomes unnecessary in understanding the behaviour of the process over time.

4.2.2 Arthur's competing technologies model

There are economic contexts in which ergodicity does not represent a necessary pre-requisite for a stochastic approach. This is the case, for example, in Arthur's competing technologies model.

Briefly, Arthur's model can be summarized as follows. Consider two increasing-returns technologies, A and B, competing passively for a market of potential adopters who are replacing an old, inferior technology. As adoptions of A (or B) increase, learning-by-using [ROSENBERG(1982)] takes place and improved versions of A (or B) become available, with correspondingly higher pay-offs or returns to those adopting them. Let us now consider two types of adopters, R and S, with 'natural' preferences for A and B respectively, and with pay-offs as in Table 4.2. Suppose each potential adopter type is equally prevalent, but that the actual 'arrivals' of R and S-agents are

---

[3] A Markov process has the property that the probability of any particular future behaviour of the process,when its current state is known exactly, is not altered by additional knowledge concerning its past behaviour. When a Markov process has stationary transition probabilities (independent of the time variable) it is called homogeneous.

	A	B
R-agent	$a_R + r\,n_A(n)$	$b_R + r\,n_B(n)$
S-agent	$a_S + s\,n_A(n)$	$b_S + s\,n_B(n)$

See ARTHUR(1983)

⋆ $n_A(n)$ and $n_B(n)$ are the number of choices of A anb B respectively, where n choices in total have been made. Due to the natural preferences of the agents $a_R > b_R$ and $b_S > a_S$.

Table 4.2: **Returns to adopting A or B**

subject to 'small unknown events' outside the model. Then all we can say is that it is equally likely that an R or an S-agent will arrive next to make their choice. Initially at least, if an R-agent arrives at the 'adoption window' to make his choice he will adopt A; if an S-agent arrives, he will adopt B. Thus the differences in adoptions between A and B move up or down with probability $1/2$.

If, by 'chance', a large number of R-types cumulates in the line of choosers, A will then be heavily adopted and hence improved in pay-off. In fact, if A gains a sufficient lead over B in adoptions, it will pay S-types to switch to A. Then both R and S types will be adopting A, and only A, from then on. The adoption process will then become locked-in to technology A. Similarly, if a sufficient number of S-types had by 'chance' arrived to adopt B over A, B would improve sufficiently to cause R-types to switch to B. The process would instead lock-in to B.

This process is a random walk with absorbing barriers on each side, the barriers corresponding to the lead in adoption it takes for each agent-type to switch its choice.

Asymptotic theory is important in showing three key features of the dynamics that arise in this non-ergodic 'increasing returns' case.

First, a priori we cannot say with accuracy which technological structure will win the market. Second, the technology that comes to dominate does not necessarily have to be the objectively 'best' or most efficient; events early on can lock the system into an inferior technological path. Third, once a single-technology structure emerges and becomes self-reinforcing, it is difficult to change it. If it were desirable to re-establish an excluded technology, an ever-widening technical change-over gap would have to be closed. For non-ergodic systems these properties — *non-predictability*, potential *non-superiority* and structural *rigidity* — appear, according to ARTHUR(1983), to be common and to some degree inevitable.

However, in Arthur's model *it is not inevitable that the process eventually become locked-into one technology.* Consider a more general case in which there is a continuum of agent types, rather than just two. We can now think of agents as distributed over adoption pay-offs. An adopter is chosen at random from this probability distribution each time a choice is to be made; and the distribution itself shifts as returns to A or B increase with an adoption of either A or B respectively. It has been shown that when returns to adoption are bounded (i.e. there is a ceiling to the increasing returns) — perhaps because learning effects eventually become exhausted — lock-in is not inevitable [see ARTHUR(1988)]. In this case, certain sequences of adopter types could bid the returns to both technologies upward more or less in concert. These technologies could then reach their 'increasing returns ceiling' together, with the adoption market shared from then on. Notwithstanding this, other adopter-arrival sequences might increase the returns of A or B early on. Thus, with increasing but bounded returns to adoption, the general finding is that some 'event histories' will lead dynamically to a shared market; other 'event histories' lead to a lock-in of the market.

This model, like all theoretical models, is obviously stylized. But it does capture an important general characteristic of competition between technologies with increasing returns. Under competitive conditions, the outcome of the process of technical change is inherently *non-predictable*; and the process can be swayed by the cumulation of 'small historical events' or small heterogeneities, or small differences in timing. As Arthur stresses, what we have in this simple model is *order* (the eventual adoption-share outcome) emerging from *fluctuation* (the inherent randomness in the arrival sequence). In modern terminology, the competing-technologies adoption process is therefore a *self-organizing* process [PRIGOGINE(1976)].

4.3   Division of labour as a stochastic process

The process of 'division of labour–technical change' can be represented by a stochastic model similar to those described above.

Randomness is introduced not only by the agent's lack of knowledge of all events that can affect the path that the process takes, but especially by the non-predictability of the outcomes. In fact, the economic system must be seen as an interrelated whole in a state of *constant and internally generated change*. Unceasing change results from the fact that the division of labour is at once a cause and an effect of economic progress. Established positions (the states of the process) are constantly under pressure, not merely because of autonomous changes in tasks and technique but also by virtue of the fact that at any point of time there will exist unexploited opportunities from the future division of labour and the consequent regrouping of operations.

A stochastic model is particularly suitable to explain how technical change is governed by its internal dynamics, at the level of a single process of production.

As in Ch.3, let us start by assuming that the process of production may be described as a sequence of m elementary operations that can be performed by men and/or machines. Moreover, let us suppose that a certain job, such as the production of a ware, is to be performed on a certain scale (q) and that for producing the quantity q, k workers are necessary. If for example $k = m = 3$, the process of production can be represented as follows:

$$
\begin{array}{llll}
a1 & b2 & c3 & \\
& a1 & b2 & c3 \\
& & etc & \cdots\cdots\cdots
\end{array}
$$

_____→

time

where worker *a* performs only operation 1, worker *b* only operation 2 and worker *c* only operation 3.

To model the impact of the division of labour on such a process of production we must take account of the three features discussed in the previous chapter:

1. the *ordering* — the division of labour proceeds by a succession of steps (subsequent increases in the number of operations performed within the productive process), each of which represents a certain increase of productivity[4] due to organizational and/or technical innovation;

2. the *element of time* — which elapses between one step and the following one and which must be regarded as a random variable, because of the unpredictability of changes.

3. the *accumulation of knowledge* — extensions of scale beyond the frontiers of current experience patently require searching for additional technological knowledge by considering the possibilities of modifying past practices and evaluating their prospective effects.

To take account of the first two features, we assume, on the one side, that the impact of the organizational and/or technological changes on the process of production may be described by a step function which changes at random points in time and always by a unit step (this is the most convenient assumption from a mathematical point of view). On the other side, time will be 'represented' by by the parameter m[5]; it will therefore be conceived as *event time*.

As far as the third feature is concerned, we will interpret it as a form of 'historical' dependence: the actual decisions are influenced by

---

[4]In accordance with the classical viewpoint, we may assume that each increase in productivity leads to a subsequent increase of scale, through a reduction of costs of production. This is possible, of course, in the presence of a suitable potential demand.

[5]It is implicit in our discussion that $\dfrac{\Delta m}{\Delta t} > 0$. We are aware that there might be cases in which the process of 'division of labour–technical change' reduces m (e.g. through mechanization of operations); however, in what follows we exclude this possibility.

the outcomes of the past decisions. The model must therefore have a 'memory' of, at least, the recent events. For this reason, we will make use of Markov models, and in addition we will introduce 'ad hoc' assumptions, in accordance with the process of economic change which we aim to describe.

In what follows we introduce two stochastic models which aim to describe the dynamic economies of scale generated by both subdivision of labour and displacement of labour within a single process of production. The division of labour is described as a random process of 'selection' between different options, which takes place through time and follows a path which is non-predictable. However, the path that the process takes influences the outcome of the process of selection, increasing (or reducing) the probabilities of occurrence of the alternative events.

We believe that the adoption of such a microperspective does not inhibit study of the phenomenon at a macro level (industry, society) later on. The link that we will highlight, in Ch.5, between the division of labour, considered as a stochastic process, on the one hand, and the progress functions, on the other hand, allows us to bring our analysis to a macro level, concentrating attention on the key elements that influence the economy's productivity performance.

4.3.1   The first model

Let us first concentrate on the subdivision of labour within a productive process, which we assume to be composed of m operations at a certain time t.

Each operation can be considered as a population of its i 'representatives', i being the number of times that the operation is performed within the process [with i less or equal to m]. Therefore the state of the process can be depicted in terms of classes of operations, characterized by different sizes. We will denote by $f(i,m)$ the number of elementary operations belonging to class i when the whole process is composed of m operations and n $[= \sum_{i=1}^{m} f(i,m)]$ the total number of elementary operations performed within the productive process. The size of class i will be denoted by the product $i f(i,m)$

[i.e. $m = \sum_{i=1}^{m} i\, f(i,m)$].

As an effect of the dynamic economies of scale generated by the subdivision of labour, the number of operations will grow. We assume that the $(m+1)th$ operation can be of two different kinds, according to the prevalence of 1)parallel-series or 2)longer-series scale economies [see Ch.3]:

1. a repetition of an operation already present in the productive process, aiming to increase the rate of utilization of workers and machines already employed in the process of production (change from class $i-1$ to class i, or from class i to class $i+1$);

2. a new elementary operation, never performed before within the process of production (addition to class 1).

The run of events will be described as the random allocation of any additional operation to one of the class-sizes which define the state of the process.

Let us illustrate with an example the definitions introduced up to now. Consider the following line of production

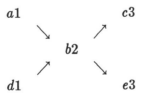

In this case we have $m = 5$, $n = 3$, $i = \{1,2\}$ with $f(1,5) = 1$ and $f(2,5) = 2$. The subdivision of labour may modify the line of production in various different ways, for instance, introducing, first, a new stage of production [$m = 6$, $n = 4$, $i = \{1,2\}$, $f(1,6) = 2$ and $f(2,6) = 2$] and then replicating it in order to utilize fully the productive capacity. Under these circumstances, the final configurations will be the following

$$a1 \qquad\qquad c3 \longrightarrow f4$$
$$\searrow \qquad \nearrow$$
$$b2$$
$$\nearrow \qquad \searrow$$
$$d1 \qquad\qquad e3 \longrightarrow g4$$

with $m = 7$, $n = 4$, $i = \{1,2\}$, $f(1,7) = 1$ and $f(2,7) = 3$.

To make clear the difference between replications and new elementary operations let us consider the following example.

Suppose two friends go fishing; we can imagine that they perform at least four separate operations: 1) to row; 2) to bait a hook; 3) to cast the fishing-line; 4) to strike the fish. Let us suppose that person A performs only the first operation and person B performs sequentially all the others.

One day one of the two friends decides to bring his son with him to teach him how to fish. While is learning the son might specialize in preparing new baits which increase the catch of fish. "To prepare new baits" is, in our perspective, a new elementary operation. It is worthwhile to stress that the emergence of a new elementary operation does not change either the nature or the allocation of the operations already performed: person A still rows, person C (the son) prepares baits and person B puts the new bait on the hook, casts the fishing-line and strikes.

Of course, if person C (or person A) starts performing some other operation - without substituting any other person - we will refer to this organizational change as a repetition.

As we stressed on various occasions, the outcome of the process of division of labour is non-predictable. In the context of our model this means that we cannot predict exactly what sort of operation will be the next. However, in accordance with the dictum 'the division of labour depends in large part upon the division of labour' [YOUNG(1928)], we may assume that the probability of an increase in the number of operations is proportional to the actual size of the process of production, namely to the number of operations which are already performed at a certain time. In particular, following

SIMON(1955)[6], we introduce the following assumptions :

1. the probability that the $(m+1)th$ operation is an operation that has been already performed exactly i times is proportional to the total number of 'representatives' of all the operations that have been performed exactly i-times [i.e. is equal to $\lambda i f(i, m)$, where λ is the factor of proportionality];

2. there is a constant probability (α) that the $(m + 1)th$ operation is a new elementary (or split-off) operation.[7]

The first assumption concerns the memory capacity of our model and corresponds to Simon's reformulation of Gibrat's law of proportionate effect.

However, in our context, the 'population law' would state that the probability that a particular operation will be the next one to be replicated is proportional to the number of its existing representatives. In fact, we make a much weaker assumption, leaving open the possibility that among all operations that are currently performed i times the probability of recurrence of some may be higher than of others.

The second assumption presupposes that the innovative process is exogenously determined, and represents the main limitation of our model, from an explanatory point of view. However, as we will see below, the constancy of α allows us to stress the role of the organizational innovations as far as the eventual behaviour of the process of division of labour is concerned, and it will be extremely important in order to connect the 'micro' analysis carried out in this chapter with the 'macro' analysis of the next chapter.

---

[6] Simon has applied this model to the study of the distribution of word frequencies in a ever-growing text. To our knowledge, no attempt has been made before to apply it to the study of dynamic increasing returns. The stochastic model used by Simon for studying the distribution of business firm sizes differs from the one under consideration, assuming that the length of the process, m, is kept constant by the simultaneous death and birth of firms.

[7] These assumptions describe a so-called linear birth process, a Markov process that is shown to apply, for example, to a population of bacteria which multiply by splitting from time to time.

Our stochastic model of division of labour[8] is described by the following system of equations:

$$f(i, m+1) - f(i, m) = \lambda\{(i-1)f(i-1, m) - i\,f(i, m)\}, \; \forall i \geq 2$$
$$\tag{4.1}$$
$$f(1, m+1) - f(1, m) = \alpha - \lambda f(1, m) \qquad (0 < \alpha < 1)$$

which says that the expected number of operations belonging to class i when the productive process will be composed of $m+1$ operations will differ from the number of operations belonging to class i when the process is composed of m operations only if there will be a number of changes from class $i-1$ to class i and/or from class i to class $i+1$.

Since $\lambda i\, f(i, m)$ is the probability that the $(m+1)th$ operation is one that is currently performed i times, we must have

$$\sum_{i=1}^{m} \lambda i\, f(i, m) = \lambda \sum_{i=1}^{m} i\, f(i, m) = 1 - \alpha$$

But

$$\sum_{i=1}^{m} i\, f(i, m) = m$$

---

[8] The formal representation of the model is derived from the 'forward' equation of a linear birth process (YULE PROCESS):

$$P_{k,n}(t+h) - P_{k,n}(t) = -\lambda\left[nP_{k,n}(t) - (n-1)P_{k,n-1}(t)\right] \qquad n \geq k$$

with the initial condition

$$P_{k,n}(0) = \begin{cases} 1 & n = k \\ 0 & n \neq k \end{cases}$$

$P_{k,n}(t)$ indicates the transition probability from state k to n in the time interval $[0, t]$. The Yule process is a special type of birth process in which the total population birth rate is directly proportional to the population size, the proportionality constant being the individual birth rate λ. The boundary condition for system (4.1) is the following:

$$f(i, 1) = \delta_{i1} = \begin{cases} 1 & i = 1 \\ 0 & i \neq 1 \end{cases}$$

Hence

$$\lambda = \frac{1 - \alpha}{m} \qquad (4.2)$$

The dependence of λ on m implies that the model, in the actual configuration, is not homogeneous. This means that the probability that the $(m+1)th$ operation is one that is currently performed i times comes to depend not only on the size of class i, as we assumed, but also by the total number of operations performed within the productive process. To find a remedy for this, we could assume, following SIMON(1955), that

$$\frac{f(i, m+1)}{f(i, m)} = \frac{m+1}{m} \quad \forall i \qquad (4.3)$$

i.e. that all the frequencies grow proportionately with m. As a consequence of this additional assumption the relative frequencies $f^*(i) = \dfrac{f(i, m)}{n}$ are independent of m :

$$\frac{f^*(i)}{f^*(i-1)} = \frac{f(i, m)}{f(i-1, m)} = \frac{f(i, m+1)}{f(i-1, m+1)} = \beta(i) \qquad (4.4)$$

Rewriting the system of equations (4.1) for $f^*(i)$ and bearing in mind (4.2), (4.3) and (4.4) we obtain

$$\left(\frac{m+1}{m} - 1\right) f(i, m) = \frac{1-\alpha}{m} \left\{ \frac{i-1}{\beta(i)} - i \right\} f(i, m)$$

Solving for $\beta(i)$, we have the following 'steady-state' solution.

$$f^*(i) = \frac{(1-\alpha)(i-1)}{1 + (1-\alpha)i} f^*(i-1) \qquad (4.5)$$

However, assumption (4.3) imposes on $f(i, m)$ a pattern of growth that can easily be shown to be inconsistent with the system of equation (4.1), because of the influence of α on $\beta(i)$ [see Appendix A]. In addition, the acceptance of such an assumption would considerably narrow the descriptive power of our model.

Indeed, we can obtain the steady-state solution (4.5) by adopting a weaker assumption than (4.3). Let us suppose that $\dfrac{f(i,m)}{m}$ tends to coincide with $f^*(i)$ for large m, in such a way that

$$\frac{f(i,m)}{m} = f^*(i) + \frac{\gamma(i)}{m} + o(\frac{1}{m}) \qquad (4.6)$$

i.e., the following limit exists

$$\lim_{m\to\infty} m \left[\frac{f(i,m)}{m} - f^*(i) \right] = \gamma(i)$$

and the rate of convergence is of order $\dfrac{1}{m}$ or faster.[9]
Introducing this condition in the model we obtain

$$(m+1)\, f^*(i) + \gamma(i) + o(1) - m\, f^*(i) - \gamma(i) + o(1) =$$
$$= (1-\alpha) \left\{ (i-1) \left[f^*(i-1) + \frac{\gamma(i-1)}{m} + o(\frac{1}{m}) \right] + \right.$$
$$\left. -i \left[f^*(i) + \frac{\gamma(i)}{m} + o(\frac{1}{m}) \right] \right\}$$

namely

$$f^*(i) + o(1) \;=\; (1-\alpha)\left\{ (i-1)\, f^*(i-1) - i\, f^*(i) + o(1) \right\}$$

For m tending to infinity the previous equation becomes

$$f^*(i) \;=\; (1-\alpha)\left\{ (i-1)\, f^*(i-1) - i\, f^*(i) \right\}$$

---

[9] The symbol o, indicates the 'order of magnitude' of a certain function. For example, a convenient way to indicate that a function $f(x)$ is of *lower order of magnitude* than a function $g(x)$ is to write $f = o(g)$, meaning that the quotient f/g has the limit 0. This notation is particularly useful for indicating the order of magnitude of the error in an approximation formula [cf. COURANT–JOHN(1965), pp.248-55].

and this expression is identical to (4.5) above. Analogously we can obtain[10]:

$$f^*(1) = \frac{\alpha}{2 - \alpha}$$

Therefore the steady-state solution for the system of equations (4.1) is the following

$$f(i, m) = \frac{(1 - \alpha)(i - 1)}{1 + (1 - \alpha)i} f(i - 1, m)$$

$$f(1, m) = \frac{n\,\alpha}{2 - \alpha}$$

(4.7)

---

[10]The value of $f^*(1)$ may be obtained as follows. From system (4.1) we know that

$$f(1, m + 1) - f(1, m) = \alpha - \lambda\, f(1, m)$$

Substituting for $f(1, m + 1)$ and $f(1, m)$ according to expression (4.6) and remembering that $\lambda = \dfrac{1 - \alpha}{m}$ we get

$$(m + 1)f^*(1) + \gamma(1) + o(1) - [mf^*(1) + \gamma(1) + o(1)] =$$
$$= \alpha - (1 - \alpha)\left[f^*(1) + \frac{\gamma(1)}{m} + o(\frac{1}{m})\right]$$

namely

$$f^*(1) + o(1) = \alpha - (1 - \alpha)\left[f^*(1) + \frac{\gamma(1)}{m} + o(\frac{1}{m})\right]$$

For $m \to \infty$ the previous equation becomes

$$f^*(1) = \alpha - (1 - \alpha)\,f^*(1)$$

namely

$$f^*(1) = \frac{\alpha}{2 - \alpha}$$

Let us provide an economic interpretation of this result, concentrating our attention on the following expression

$$\frac{f(i,m)}{f(i-1,m)} = \frac{(1-\alpha)(i-1)}{1+(1-\alpha)i} = \beta(i,\alpha) \qquad (4.8)$$

which says that the behaviour of $f(i,m)$, for a given m, depends on the magnitude on i and α. In the context of our model, this means that the number of elementary operations which compose class i, when the size of the process of production is m, will differ from the number of operations which compose class $i-1$ according to the kind of economies of scale which predominates. In fact, recalling the definitions of α and i, we can interpret α as an indicator of the innovative activity (longer-series economies of scale) and the magnitude of i as an index of the diffusion of parallel-series economies of scale.

Partially differentiating $\beta(i,\alpha)$ — supposing that i is continuous — we obtain

$$\frac{\partial \beta(i,\alpha)}{\partial i} = \frac{(1-\alpha)(2-\alpha)}{[1+(1-\alpha)i]^2} \geq 0 \qquad (4.9)$$

and

$$\frac{\partial \beta(i,\alpha)}{\partial \alpha} = \frac{1-i}{[1+(1-\alpha)i]^2} \leq 0 \qquad (4.10)$$

These two features of the model [see FIG.4.1] can be explained as follows. According to our description of the process of division of labour and of the economies of scale which it generates, innovations are alternative and complementary to the subsequent replication of operations already performed in the productive process — aiming to utilize fully the productive capacity. As a consequence of this, the more α increases the less likely is it that the $(m+1)th$ operation will be a replication of an operation belonging to class i (for every i greater or equal to 2). Therefore, the differences in size among the various classes will tend to become smaller and smaller and, in the extreme case that $\alpha = 1$ (predominance of longer-series economies of scale), all the operations will be concentrated in class 1.

The opposite situation — the predominance of the parallel-series economies of scale — is represented by the case of large i. From

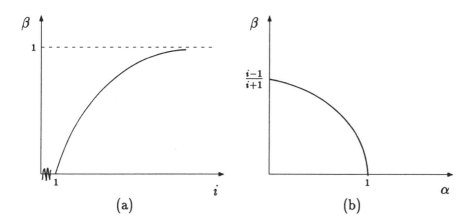

Figure 4.1: **Relationships between α, β and i**

an economic point of view a large i means that the process of production consists mainly of repetitions of some operations. From (4.7)
we derive that, in the extreme case that i is infinitely large, $f(i, m) =$
$f(i - 1, m) = 1$, i.e. all the operations performed in the process of
production are replications of two elementary operations. However,
it must be noted that, in normal conditions i.e. with a given finite
m, i cannot be infinitely large because of the constraint $i < m$. The
predominance of parallel-series economies of scale represented by the
following set of conditions

$$
\left\{
\begin{array}{rcl}
m & = & (i-1)\,f(i-1,m) + i\,f(i,m) \\
f(i,m) & = & f(i-1,m) \\
i & \leq & m
\end{array}
\right.
$$

consists therefore in the concentration of the m operations — i.e.
$f(i, m) = 1$ — in the 'central' classes $\dfrac{m+1}{2}$ and $\dfrac{m}{2}$. Of course, when
$m \to \infty$ these classes become infinitely large.

   Let us now study the behaviour of the model for large i, considering simultaneously the influence of α. If for convenience we introduce
$\rho = \dfrac{1}{1-\alpha}$ $(1 \leq \rho \leq \infty)$, we obtain

$$\beta(i, \alpha) \ = \ \frac{(i-1)}{i+\rho}$$

and

$$f^*(i) \ = \ \frac{i-1}{i+\rho} f^*(i-1)$$

By recurrent substitution we obtain [see Appendix A for details]

$$
\begin{aligned}
f^*(i) \ &= \ \beta(i)\beta(i-1) \cdots \beta(2)\, f^*(1) \ = \\
&= \ \frac{(i-1)\,(i-2)\,\cdots\,3\,2\,1}{(i+\rho)\,(i-1+\rho)\,\cdots\,(2+\rho)}\, f^*(1) \ = \\
&= \ \frac{\Gamma(i)\,\Gamma(2+\rho)}{\Gamma(i+1+\rho)}\, f^*(1) \ = \\
&= \ (\rho+1)\, f^*(1)\, B(\rho+1, i)
\end{aligned}
$$

where $B(\rho+1, i)$ is a complete Beta distribution with parameters i and $\rho+1$. If we take $A = (\rho+1)\, f^*(1)$ we can write

$$f^*(i) = A\, B(\rho+1, i) \tag{4.11}$$

This is the Yule distribution, a highly skewed distribution with very long upper tails, that can be approximated[11] by a function of the form

---

[11]It is a well-known property of the Gamma function that as $i \to \infty$, and for any constant k.

$$\Gamma(i)/\Gamma(i+k) \ \sim \ i^{-k}$$

Hence

$$f^*(i) \ \sim \ \Gamma(\rho+2) i^{(\rho+1)}$$

where $\Gamma(\rho+2)$ and $(\rho+1)$ are constant.

$$f^*(i) = a\,i^{-k} \qquad (4.12)$$

where a, k are constant. In the present case $a = \Gamma(\rho+2)$ and $k = \rho+1$.
This distribution is known in the economic literature as the Pareto
distribution and it has been shown to fit the size distribution of various kinds of social aggregates: personal wealth, incomes and business
firms [see STEINDL(1965)]. According to ZIPF(1949), this distribution is generated by the balance of two opposing forces: the forces of
'Diversification' and 'Unification'. In our model, these two forces take
the forms of the increasing subdivision of labour, on the one side, and
of the re-grouping of operations, on the other side. Moreover, the appearance of the Pareto distribution can be interpreted as a regularity
of the process of subdivision of labour, emerging from the 'chaos' of
the random changes.

4.3.2   The second model

The model described above has concentrated on the intra-firm process
of subdivision of labour. It is now time to consider also the displacement of labour, i.e. the dynamic substitution of workers by machines
in the performance of very simplified operations.

In the next model, leaving aside the re-grouping of operations
caused by the parallel-series economies of scale, we describe the increasing intra-firm division of labour as both further specialization
of labour and progressive mechanization of routine operations. As
in the previous model, we assume that the actual division of labour
depends on the previous division of labour, i.e. the changes of state
are influenced by the path that the process takes. However, in the
present case, changes take place in continuous time, whereas, in the
previous model, we have adopted, for sake of simplicity, discrete and
operational time.

Let us concentrate on just a portion of the production process
consisting, at time t, of M (= constant) elementary operations —
rendered apparent by a previous subdivision of labour — which may
be either of type A or of type B [A-type = operations performed by
men, B-type = operations performed by machines]. If we assume that

the state of the process $X(t)$ represents the number of A-type operations at time t, the development of the state in time will be described
by a step function which changes at random points in time and always
by a unit step, either up or down, according to which direction the
division of labour takes [automation or further specialization].

The changes in the structure of the process of production are ef-
fected as follows.

First of all, one of the M elementary operations which compose
the portion of the productive process under consideration, is selected
to be replaced. If $X(t) = J$ an A-type operation will be selected
to be replaced with probability $\dfrac{J}{M}$. We refer to this stage as death.
Next, another selection is made randomly to determine the type of the
new operation replacing the one that 'dies'. We refer to this stage as
birth. In economic terms, this means that the agent who is in charge
of organizing the production (e.g. the capitalist), in an interval of
time $(t, t + \Delta t)$, first decides to re-organize a certain activity and
then chooses one of the possible options. If the number of workers
employed in routine operations is relatively high compared with the
number of machines, it will be likely that the capitalist decides to
replace a worker with a machine. However, he might alternatively
decide to employ a 'cheaper' worker (e.g. a trainee) and postpone
the purchase of the machine. Moreover, he could take a first decision
and rapidly correct it before time $t + \Delta t$ is reached. The model may
easily admit the possibility that the type of the new operation is
altered after birth. Specifically, let γ_1 denote the probability that a
A-type mutates to a B-type and let γ_2 denote the probability that
a B-type mutates into an A-type. The conditional probability that
$X(t + \Delta t) - X(t) = -1$, when a change of state occurs, is

$$\frac{J}{M}\left[\left(1 - \frac{J}{M}\right)(1 - \gamma_2) + \frac{J}{M}\gamma_1\right] \tag{4.13}$$

where $X(t) = J$.

We deduce this formula as follows. The probability that an A-type
operation is selected to be replaced is $\dfrac{J}{M}$. Moreover, the probability
that the new operation is a B-type and that no mutation occurs is

$(1 - \dfrac{J}{M})(1 - \gamma_2)$, whereas the probability that the new operation is at first an A-type and then mutates into a B-type is $\dfrac{J}{M}\gamma_1$. The combination of these probabilities gives (4.13).

In a similar way we find that the conditional probability that $X(t + \Delta t) - X(t) = 1$ when a change of state occurs is

$$(1 - \frac{J}{M})\,[\frac{J}{M}(1 - \gamma_1) + (1 - \frac{J}{M})\,\gamma_2] \qquad (4.14)$$

The stochastic process described is a birth and death process with a finite number of states $0, 1, 2, \cdots, M$, and it can be regarded as the continuous analog of a random walk.[12]

In our model the birth and death rates are

$$\lambda_j = \lambda(1 - \frac{J}{M})\,[\frac{J}{M}(1 - \gamma_1) + (1 - \frac{J}{M})\,\gamma_2]$$

$$(4.15)$$

$$\mu_j = \mu\,(\frac{J}{M})\,[\frac{J}{M}\gamma_1 + (1 - \frac{J}{M})\,(1 - \gamma_2)]$$

The general importance of birth and death processes as models derives in large part from the availability of standard formulas for studying the limiting behaviour of such processes. For a birth and death process without absorbing states (i.e., $\lambda_o \neq 0$ — see Appendix

---

[12]Indicating with $P_{ij}(t)$ the stationary transition probabilities [i.e., $P_{ij}(t) = Pr\{X(t + h) = j \mid X(h) = i\}$, $\forall\, h \geq 0$], the birth and death process is described by the following system of differential equations (Kolmogorov forward equations)

$$P'_{i,k}(t) = \lambda_{k-1}P_{i,k-1}(t) + \mu_{k+1}P_{i,k+1}(t) - (\lambda_k + \mu_k)P_{i,k}(t)$$
$$P'_{i,0}(t) = -\lambda_0 P_{i,0}(t) + \mu_1 P_{i,1}(t)$$

with the initial conditions

$$P_{i,k}(0) = \delta_{i,k} = \begin{cases} 1 & i = k \\ 0 & i \neq k \end{cases}$$

A for details), like the one that we are dealing with, it can be proved that a limiting distribution $\{\Pi_k\}_{k=0}^{M}$ exists and it is stationary in that

$$\Pi_k = \sum_{i=0}^{M} \Pi_i \, P_{ik}$$

which tells us that if the process starts in state i with probability Π_i, then at any time it will be in state i with the same probability Π_i.[13]

It is interesting to see what happens to the stationary limiting distribution of our model when $M \to \infty$ and the probabilities of 'mutation' γ_1 and γ_2 tend to zero in such a way that $\gamma_1 M \to k_1$ and $\gamma_2 M \to k_2$, where $0 < k_1, k_2 < \infty$ are constants. It can be shown [see KARLIN–TAYLOR(1984), pp.238-40] that the stationary limiting distribution $\{\Pi_k\}_{k=0}^{M}$ becomes, for $M \to \infty$, a Beta distribution with parameters k_1, k_2. Recalling that the Yule distribution has a density function proportional to a complete Beta, also in this case we can plausibly approximate the stationary limiting distribution with a Pareto distribution, or with a distribution whose tail has this form.

4.4   Conclusions

The aim of this chapter was to deal with the process of dynamic increasing returns generated by the intra-firm division of labour. For this purpose, we have introduced two stochastic models of division of labour, which present the following common characteristics:

- the division of labour is described as a random process of 'selection' between different options, which takes place through time and follows a path which is non-predictable;

---

[13]The probabilities $\{\Pi_k\}_{k=0}^{M}$ can be derived from the forward equations passing to the limit as $t \to \infty$ and solving the resulting system of equations [see KARLIN–TAYLOR(1984), pp.232-3]. The solution gives

$$\Pi_k = \frac{\theta_k}{\sum_{k=0}^{M} \theta_k} \quad k = 0, 1, \cdots, M$$

where $\theta_k = \dfrac{\lambda_0 \lambda_1 \cdots \lambda_{k-1}}{\mu_1 \mu_2 \cdots \mu_k}$ and $\theta_0 = 1$

- the path that the process takes (i.e. the previous organizational and technical changes) influences the outcome of the process of selection, increasing (or reducing) the probabilities of occurrence of the alternative events;

- the long-run behaviour of the process of division of labour shows the emergence of regularity (in the form of a Pareto function), from the 'chaos' of random outcomes. In other words, despite its random nature, the intra-firm division of labour gives rise to a balanced sequence of organizational and technical changes and, in this way, causes a steady increase of productivity.

In comparison with Arthur's competing technologies model, our models are extremely elementary, and do not allow general considerations about 'potential non-superiority' or 'structural rigidity' of the process of increasing returns. However, as in Arthur's case, our models are path-dependent and indeed they prove to be very similar to two classes of models which ARTHUR(1987) names 'allocation processes' and 'recontracting processes'.[14]

Both these classes of dynamic models are of a 'self-reinforcing' type and tend to possess a multiplicity of asymptotic states. The initial starting state and random events influence the convergence of the model to one of these asymptotic states and thus 'select the structure that the system eventually locks into'.

The more 'standard' asymptotic behaviour of our models depends on some specific assumptions that we have introduced [about α and $f(i,m)$ in the first model and about γ_1 and γ_2 in the second model] to control the direction of the processes involved. We have opted for a loss of generality in favour of a description of the process of division

---

[14]On the one side, allocation processes have the following characteristics: 1) a unit addition (or allocation) is made to one of K categories at each time, with probabilities that are a function of the proportion of units currently in the K categories; 2) time is event time, not clock time; 3) the models study how the proportions in each category build up. On the other side recontracting processes can be described as follows: 1) they assume a total allocation of fixed size T divided among K categories, and transitions between categories (e.g. of one unit at a time) are possible with probabilities that depend on the numbers of units in each category; 2) time is, generally, clock time; 3) the models study the evolution of the probability of finding the process at a certain state at a certain time. For the algebra see ARTHUR(1987).

of labour as close as possible to the classical viewpoint described in the previous chapters. The emergence of the Pareto function, in both cases, fits in well with the classical idea of a 'balanced' modification of a given process of production introduced by the progressive division of labour [see Ch.2].

However, the microperspective here adopted and the lack of consideration for the endogenous nature of the innovative activity, due to the assumptions on which the two models are based, do not allow our models fully to represent the classical viewpoint. In order to analyse the link between increasing productivity and growth of output, as well as to explore the consequences of the division of labour in terms of behaviour of the firm and different market forms, we must combine the present analysis with a macroperspective, which considers the economic system as an interrelated whole. This will be the object of the following chapters.

5 Division of labour and progress functions

5.1 Introduction

In the previous chapter we have described the random character of the industrial division of labour and introduced two stochastic models of intra-firm division of labour. In this chapter, the analysis is enlarged to consider the various interdependences and feedbacks that characterize the process of economic growth based on division of labour and technical change.

In this 'macro' context, we make use of a well-known deterministic model — the progress function[1] — to describe the 'circular causation' between output and labour productivity ($\frac{Q}{L}$): on the one hand, output growth causes — through an increasing division of labour — a reduction of labour input, i.e. growth of productivity; on the other hand, productivity growth results in a fall of prices relative to wages

---

[1]The phenomenon under examination has been variously termed as 'learning curve', 'progress function', 'improvement curve', 'experience curve', 'efficiency curve' etc. . In particular, the name 'learning curve' strongly implies that all productivity improvement, when equipment is kept constant, is due to increased operative skills. In fact, improvement with production experience may be attributed both to 'operative' and 'management' factors, e.g. increased management efficiency in work scheduling, introduction of superior methods of production,etc..See STEEDMAN(1967).

and thereby stimulates both demand and output.

In the light of the classical theory, first we introduce some modifications to the form of the model (as far as the coefficient of the progress function is concerned), apt to emphasize the role of the flow of innovations (organizational, managerial and technical) to which the division of labour gives rise. Secondly, we 'merge' it with Sraffa's model to consider the industrial operations as an interrelated whole.

5.2 The progress function theory

5.2.1 A brief review and a criticism

The concept of progress (or improvement) function is that *labour input per unit of product declines as cumulative output increases*. Mathematically, this can be expressed as follows (log-linear 'unit' curve):

$$l_N = l_1 N^{-b} \tag{5.1}$$

where

N : cumulative total of units produced;
l_N : hours of direct labour employed on the Nth unit;
l_1 : hours of direct labour employed in the production of the first unit;
b : progress elasticity.

The general principle is that improvements in the utilization of a given technique do not become available from the passage of time as such but are a product of experience. If experience can be measured by the cumulative amount of a commodity produced, then the higher is production, the greater will be the opportunities for improvements.

Born as a short term relation holding under constant conditions in an industrial plant[2], the progress function has been subsequently

---

[2]There are various possible specifications of the progress function:

- GLOVER (1965) : $l(N) = l_1 N^{1-b}$, where $l(N)$ is the total quantity of direct labour expended in the manufacture of the first N units of production.

- WRIGHT (1936) : $Al_N = l_1 N^{-b}$, where $Al_N = \frac{l(N)}{N}$.

incorporated into the main corpus of economic theory, mainly owing to the works of Arrow, Verdoorn and Kaldor [see ARROW (1962), VERDOORN (1949), (1956), KALDOR (1957), (1966), KALDOR-MIRRLEES(1962)].

According to Arrow, new machines are the vehicle of technical progress (vintage approach), i.e. labour input (per unit of output) on new machines falls over time as experience permits a better design of machines. Consequently, Arrow takes 'experience' to be measured by the cumulative gross investment (cumulative production of capital goods) in the economy rather than by the cumulative output.

Kaldor and Mirrlees' treatment of technical progress is also based on the vintage approach. They modify the technical progress function[3], introduced by KALDOR(1957), expressing the rate of increase of output per man on the latest machine as an increasing function of the rate of increase of investment per man (rather than of the cumulative gross investment as in Arrow). The technical progress function is non-linear, showing a diminishing rate of response of productivity increase to investment increase. The underlying notion is that technical change has two elements: an exogenous increase in ideas, and the extension and exploitation of these ideas by 'learning'. More investment permits the stock of ideas currently available to be more throughly explored and developed, but there are limits to their potentialities; hence the diminishing response of the growth of productivity to investment increase.

- DE JONG (1957), (1964) : $l_N = l_\infty + (l_1 - l_\infty)N^{-b}$, where l_∞, is the positive minimum value for l_N, or $l_N = l_1[M + (1 - M)N^{-b}]$ where $M = \frac{l_\infty}{l_1}$, $0 \le M \le 1$.

[3]In its original form Kaldor's technical progress function was conceived as a relationship between the rate of growth of labour productivity (measured as the annual percentage growth in output per worker) and the rate of growth of capital per worker (annual percentage). The focus of attention was explicitly the mutual relationship between accumulation of capital and technical progress. However, since, under continuous technical progress and obsolescence, there is no way of measuring the 'stock of capital', KALDOR-MIRRLEES(1962) avoids 'the notion of a quantity of capital, and its corollary, the rate of capital accumulation, as variables of the system; it operates solely with the value of current gross investment (gross fixed capital expenditure per unit of time) and its rate of change in time'(p.174).

On the empirical side, VERDOORN(1949) argues that there is a positive correlation between productivity growth and output growth[4] and that the elasticity of labour productivity with respect to output proves to be constant in the long run[5]. Referring to a 'macro' level (i.e. to an industry or to the economic system as a whole) the relationship is usually specified in the following form:

$$\hat{\pi} = a + b\,\hat{q} \qquad (5.2)$$

where
$\hat{\pi}$: rate of growth of productivity;
$\hat{q}$: rate of growth of output;
a and b are constant and b, according to Verdoorn, is in the region of one-half.

Considering that $\hat{\pi} = \hat{q} - \hat{L}$, the above equation may be specified alternatively as:

$$\hat{L} = c + d\,\hat{q} \qquad (5.3)$$

where d is still in the region of one-half. The latter specification of the law has been proposed by KALDOR(1966) and it is indeed preferable

---

[4]Indeed, Verdoorn's proposition is nothing but a modified version of Smith's theorem. In Verdoorn's words, 'one could have expected a priori to find a correlation between labour productivity and output, given that the division of labour only comes about through increases in the volume of production; therefore the expansion of production creates the possibility of further rationalisation which has the same effects as mechanisation' [VERDOORN(1949), p.4; English translation in THIRLWALL(1980), p.388].

[5]Verdoorn refers to the 'normal assumptions of long-period analysis' meaning that the growth rates of the variables concerned are assumed approximately constant, and therefore that 'their period-averages are roughly representative of what is currently called the steady-state of the system' [VERDOORN(1980), p.382]. Under these assumptions the elasticity of labour productivity with respect to output can be defined as follows:

$$\eta = \frac{\frac{d(q/L)}{dt}/\frac{q}{L}}{\hat{q}/q} = \left(\frac{L}{q}\right)\frac{L\hat{q}-\dot{L}q}{L^2} = 1 - \frac{\dot{L}/L}{\hat{q}/q}$$

Therefore the constancy of η implies the constancy of the ratio $\frac{\dot{L}/L}{\hat{q}/q}$, i.e. of the elasticity of labour with respect to output.

since it avoids the spurious correlation due to the presence of q on both sides of the equation.[6]

It is important to stress that the Verdoorn–Kaldor equation may be derived from a progress function defined as

$$\pi \;=\; k \left(\int_0^t q_t \, dt \right)^b$$

where $\left(\int_0^t q_t \, dt \right)$ is the cumulative output defined in continuous time. Assuming that $q_t = q_o \, e^{\varsigma t}$ [see VERDOORN(1956)] we can substitute this value for q_t and solving the integral we obtain

$$\pi \;=\; k \left(\frac{q_t - q_o}{\varsigma} \right)^b$$

As t becomes large, π will approach the expression

$$\pi \;=\; k \, \varsigma^{-b} \, q^b$$

which is equivalent to (5.2) above.

For this reason we regard Verdoorn's expression as the 'macro' equivalent of the 'micro' log-linear progress function (5.1).

Both the micro and the macro formulations of the progress function present as a distinctive characteristic the constancy of the progress elasticity. A constant b is empirically observed both at plant level, with given techniques [according to WRIGHT(1936), for example, $b = 1/3$], and at 'macro' level, under long-period assumptions [Verdoorn's coefficient $= 1/2$].[7]

As a result, a theoretical explanation of how the exponent of the progress function is determined, is generally lacking. This deficiency, together with other limitations that concern the empirical use of the progress function, are behind the criticisms made against this analytical tool [see STEEDMAN(1967), SAHAL(1975) and STEINDL(1980)].

---

[6] The specification of the Verdoorn–Kaldor law has not been without its critics [see WOLFE(1968), ROWTHORN(1975),(1979), McCOMBIE(1981),(1982)]; however, no criticism has been shown to be irrefutable or necessarily damaging.

[7] In Arrow's analysis the constancy of b is assumed on the basis of the 'micro' empirical results. The aggregation problem which shows that a 'macro' relationship may significantly depart from the underlying individual relationships is ignored.

In the following pages an attempt is made to describe the process giving rise to a progress function in term of a probabilistic mechanism, similar to the one previously described in our stochastic models of division of labour.

5.2.2 A stochastic interpretation

Let us write the progress function (5.1) in the form:

$$N = g\, l_N^{-h} \qquad\qquad (5.4)$$

with $g = l_1^{1/b}$ and $h = 1/b$.

It should be noted that the case of decline in the performance of the economic system is irrelevant to the theoretical concept of the progress function. This is not to deny that there exist situations where, for some reasons, increase in cumulative output is accompanied by decline in the performance. It is rather to indicate that the progress function does not explain such cases. Thus, by definition, in the above expression N increases monotonically with decreasing l_N.

Recalling the description of the process of division of labour given in the previous chapter, we know that, as an effect of the division of labour, it is possible to study systematically (as in the time and motion studies) the process of production, identifying the ability and strength necessary to optimize each individual performance. It is plausible to assume that, owing to this study, different products can be ranked according to the labour required for their production. However, these ranks must be considered as random variables, given that, in the process of division of labour, there exists an implicit random element in the way that changes in skill and productivity take place through time.

In general, then, the cumulative total of units produced (N) may be considered as *the total number of product quantities requiring at least l_N amount of labour* (per unit), i.e. be interpreted as the event $\{E > l_N\}$, where E is the rank stochastic variable.   Considering $Pr\{E \geq l_N\} = 1 - F(l_N)$ and expressing it in the form $\dfrac{E}{E^*}$, we can rewrite (5.4) in the form:

$$\frac{E}{E^*} = 1 - F(l_N) = \gamma l_N^{-h} \quad where \quad \gamma = \frac{g}{E^*} \qquad (5.5)$$

namely

$$F(l_N) = 1 - \gamma l_N^{-h} = Pr\{E < l_N\} \qquad (5.6)$$

This formulation of the progress function is isomorphic to the distribution function of the Pareto distribution:

$$F(x) = Pr\{X < x\} = 1 - a\,x^{-k} \qquad (5.7)$$

where x is a known positive number and $k \in R_+$, the positive real line.[8]

Therefore, we may consider a progress function as a manifestation of an underlying 'Paretian' phenomenon. In particular, recalling the analysis carried out in the previous chapter, we may consider the progress function as a 'technological structure' — in Arthur's terminology — emerging from the random process of division of labour. The organizational and technical changes connected with the increasing division of labour give rise to a self-reinforcing (random) process of economic growth. [Randomness being introduced — see previous chapter — mainly by the non-predictability of the path which the process of change takes.] However, in the long run[9] (i.e., at macro level, for a large cumulative output and, at a micro level, for a large process of production) a trajectory emerges and, at both macro and micro level, takes the form of a Pareto distribution (see FIG. 5.1).

From an empirical point of view, to accept this probabilistic interpretation of the progress function means to assume that the observed

---

[8] *Nota bene*: for each value of k, $f(x, k)$ represent a different density as is shown in FIG. 5.1.

[9] Empirically, the progress functions are often found to have persisted over long periods of time [see SAHAL(1981)].As an example, the relationship between improvement in the maximum tractor horsepower and cumulated tractor production during the time period 1920-71 obeys a progress function. Likewise, the decline in manhours per barrel refined in the U.S. petroleum industry since 1860 obeys a progress function with a constant exponent over a period covering more than a century. In a machine-pace operation, for instance, the progress function was found to have persisted over a long time during which tens of millions of units were produced.

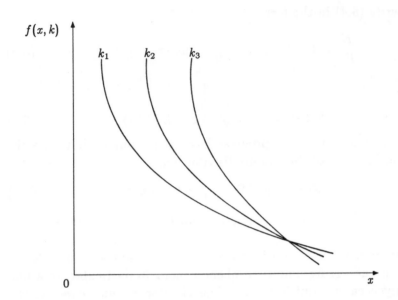

Figure 5.1: **Density function of a Pareto distribution for different values of** k

data are generated by the chance mechanism described by the density function of the Pareto distribution. The original uncertainty relating to the outcome of the process of division of labour is transformed into the uncertainty relating to the selection of the parameter k', which determines uniquely the one density, that is, $f(x, k')$, which gives rise to the observed data. [For the task of determining the unknown parameter or testing hypotheses about it using observed data, see SPANOS(1986)].

From (5.4), (5.6) and (5.7) we obtain

$$k = \frac{1}{b}$$

Therefore to determine k' is equivalent to estimating the value of the progress elasticity (or Verdoorn's coefficient, at macro level), and the constancy of b is consistent with k assuming a specific value k'.

Now, bearing in mind our stochastic models of division of labour, let us try to provide a possible interpretation of b.

From the model of intra-firm division of labour

$$f(i, m+1) - f(i, m) = \lambda[(i-1)f(i-1, m) - if(i, m)], \quad i \geq 2$$
$$f(1, m+1) - f(1, m) = \alpha - \lambda f(1, m)$$

with solution $f^*(i) = A\,B(\rho+1, i) \longrightarrow Ci^{-(\rho+1)}$ for $i \to \infty$ where $\rho = \dfrac{1}{1-\alpha}$ $[1 \leq \rho \leq \infty]$, we derive the following expression for k:

$$k = \rho + 1 = \frac{1}{1-\alpha} + 1 = \frac{2-\alpha}{1-\alpha}$$

Therefore we obtain:

$$b = \frac{1-\alpha}{2-\alpha} \tag{5.8}$$

i.e., the constancy of the progress elasticity is a consequence of the independence of what we could call the 'innovation ratio', α, from economic factors. Recalling that $0 < \alpha < 1$, according to expression (5.8) the progress elasticity takes values $1/2, 1/3$ and 0 for α equal to $0, 1/2$ and 1 respectively. Therefore the domain of b, so defined, is consistent with the observed empirical values.

Bearing in mind that expression (5.3) is valid only at 'micro' level — given that the models described in the previous chapter refer to the division of labour within a single process of production — this numerical result can be interpreted as follows. The progress function describes a process of improvement through practice which does not involve, borrowing Marshall's expression, 'any economies that may result from substantive new inventions' [MARSHALL(1920), p.461]. On the one hand, this is shown by the fact that in the case of predominance of longer-series economies of scale (i.e. $\alpha = 1, b = 0$) the progress function reduces to the form

$$\hat{\pi} = a$$

i.e. the growth of productivity is considered exogenously determined. On the other hand, this interpretation is consistent with the fact that

the most commonly observed value for b is $1/3$, and this value corresponds to an 'average' situation $(\alpha = 1/2)$ where the emergence of
longer-series and parallel-series economies of scale is equally possible.

This interpretation of the progress elasticity as an 'average innovation ratio' (say, $\bar{\alpha}$), in our view, may pave the way for identifying
the factors which influence the response of productivity growth to increases in the scale of production. In the next section, a functional
relationship linking $\bar{\alpha}$ to the rate of growth of output, $\hat{q}$, will be described and its implications further discussed.

5.3   The innovative process

The role of experience in technological change has many facets. First,
as exemplified by the progress function, a process of improvement
through practice is involved in the use of a given technology. A second,
and potentially more important, aspect of the phenomenon is that experience is a key factor underlying the introduction of innovations (not
necessarily embodied in capital goods). We have already stressed on
various occasions the classical point of view on this subject. However,
it is worthwhile to recall that the link between division of labour and
the innovative process mainly concerns 'minor' innovations, which exploit and develop the potentialities of 'major' innovations.[10] We refer
in particular to the flow of organizational, managerial and technical
innovations to which, according to Babbage, the division of labour
gives rise.

If our interpretation of the progress function — as a long-run representation of the stochastic process of reduction of labour inputs due
to the division of labour — is accepted, this flow of innovations can
be explicitly considered as one of the factors determining the 'circular causation' between growth of productivity and growth of output
(i.e. dynamic increasing returns). This opportunity is offered by in-
terpreting the coefficient of the progress function as an 'average innovation ratio', generalizing the 'micro' results discussed in the previous

---

[10]Major innovations (i.e. changes in the prevailing technologies and in the structure of employment) are here considered as the result of a unique set of institutional,
social and economic changes,i.e. of an interaction mechanism which goes beyond
the purely economic sphere.

section.[11]

It seems reasonable to suppose that demand expansion will stimulate the flow of innovations. More specifically we may relate the average innovation ratio to the rate of growth of output; the functional form of this relationship might be the following:

$$\bar{\alpha} = \alpha_\infty \, exp[-exp(A - B \, \hat{q})] \qquad (5.9)$$

with A and B constant and positive.

This is the well-known Gompertz function, an asymmetrical S-shaped curve that, among other applications, seems to represent the characteristic behaviour of many leading and innovating industries [see PRESCOTT(1922) and KUZNETS(1930)].

Let us consider in detail the elements of equation (5.9) — the saturation level (α_∞), the rate of growth of output ($\hat{q}$) and the coefficient B.

One central feature of the proposed formulation is that the relative rate of change of $\bar{\alpha}$ with respect to $\hat{q}$ decreases exponentially with $\hat{q}$[12]:

---

[11]*Nota bene*: the above functional relationship (5.8) is not general enough to constitute a proper expression of the link between the progress elasticity and the innovative process, mainly because the variable α represents just one source of innovations, those which are connected to the intra-firm subdivision of labour. Nevertheless, in our view, it offers a plausible (and useful) economic explanation of the coefficient of the progress function.

[12]It can be shown that N — and therefore $\hat{q}$ — can be regarded as a measure of time (operational time). Considering the total cumulative direct labour used in the manufacture of the first N units of production we have:

$$L(N) = l_1 \sum_{i=1}^{N} i^{-b}$$

and using an integral approximation [as is usually done in empirical studies; cf. CONWAY–SCHULTZ(1959)]

$$L(N) = \frac{l_1}{1-b} N^{1-b}$$

Let us, for the sake of argument, assume that the rate of input of labour is constant in time so that the cumulative direct labour input is L_t. Inserting that for $L(N)$ we can calculate the cumulative output as a function of time:

$$\frac{d\bar{\alpha}}{d\hat{q}}/\bar{\alpha} \;=\; B\left[exp(A - B\,\hat{q})\right]$$

and considering that

$$ln(\alpha_\infty/\bar{\alpha}) \;=\; exp(A - B\,\hat{q})$$

we can rewrite the expression of the rate of change in the form

$$\frac{d\bar{\alpha}}{d\hat{q}}/\bar{\alpha} \;=\; B\left(ln\,\alpha_\infty - ln\,\bar{\alpha}\right)$$

Therefore the greater the value of B, the greater is the relative rate of change of $\bar{\alpha}$ (given the ratio $\alpha_\infty/\bar{\alpha}$).

Having in mind the classical conceptualization of the process of 'division of labour–technical change', (see Chapters 2 and 3) the economic explanation of this functional relationship is quite straightforward. The introduction of innovations, subsequent to an increase in demand, is 'bounded' by the structural characteristics of the system of production (prevailing technologies). Moreover, it is plausible to assume that their average rate of adoption will be slow at first, but will become rapid as soon as the relevant know-how for their use is acquired. It will reach a saturation point as the opportunities for their application are exhausted (i.e. in the absence of major structural changes).[13]

The presence of the constant B indicates that other factors, apart from the expansion of the demand, can influence the innovative process. In fact, certain innovations are the result of scientific developments that are largely (though never completely) independent of economic factors; other innovations are stimulated in their appearance or

$$N_t = \left[\frac{(1-b)L_t}{l_1}\right]^{1/(1-b)} \qquad 0 < b < 1$$

It follows that the output per unit of time N_t of a given labour force is a function of t [see STEINDL(1980)].

[13]Major innovations give rise to new methods of production and represent 'breaks' in the path of innovation (broken line on the top of the graph). This implies a shift of the saturation level α_∞ :

in their expansion by some aspects of investment activity. Still other innovations are directly or indirectly stimulated by the behaviour of costs and in particular of labour cost: if this increases, the stimulus arises — or is enhanced — to introduce labour saving innovations. All these factors interact in determining the progress elasticity and consequently the productivity performance of the system of production. However, in the context of the present model, their influence is considered as exogenous and constant.

5.4 'The division of labour depends on the division of labour'

5.4.1 A Sraffa–like production model

As we stressed on previous occasions, according to the classical viewpoint the division of labour is at once a cause and an effect of economic progress. This is the basis for studying the feedback relationship between productivity growth and the growth of output: an increasing division of labour will result in a fall of prices, this will stimulate both demand and output and consequently will lead to a subsequent increase of productivity. As YOUNG(1928) stresses, this 'mechanism of increasing returns is not to be discussed adequately by observing these effects of variations in the size of an individual firm or of a particular industry, for the progressive division and specialization of industries is an essential part of the process by which increasing returns are realised. What is required is that industrial operations be

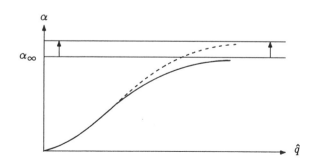

seen as an interrelated whole'(p.539). Among the theoretical models which consider industrial operations as an interrelated whole, the most promising is, in our view, that of Sraffa.

Let us consider the simplest case: two commodities, no fixed capital, no land as a constraint, a single technique, and a single product for each industry. Assuming a unique rate of profit (r) we have

$$(A_a p_a + B_a p_b)(1 + r) + L_a w = A p_a$$

$$(5.10)$$

$$(A_b p_a + B_b p_b)(1 + r) + L_b w = B p_b$$

As is well known, in *Production of Commodities by means of Commodities* the Sraffian choice of variables to be analysed is based on the relations that exist between prices of production and the distributive variables at a given point in time. Everything else (technology, levels of production) is taken as given for the analysis of the particular problem chosen. However, this choice does not represent an 'a priori' refusal to consider the possibility of analysing the problems of technical change, the determination of the levels of production[14] or the decision-making policies of firms. On the contrary, in this way, theoretical investigation may concentrate attention on the 'virtual' movement of specific variables and on the relations between these variables, as if they were being 'isolated in a vacuum'.

As far as our analysis is concerned, the variables on which we must focus attention are those most directly related with the process of 'division of labour–technical change', i.e. labour inputs, produced inputs and final output. For this reason, in the following pages, we always consider the distributive variable, r, as given; moreover we set $w = 1$ and we indicate with p_i the labour-commanded prices.

---

[14]Referring in particular to the assumption of given levels of production, RONCAGLIA(1978) argues that it is possible to show the compatibility of Sraffa's system with the recognition of the possibility of Keynesian unemployment equilibrium (under-full capacity utilization of plant, equipment and labour). Actually, there is nothing in the Sraffian system to ensure that the number of workers required by the given levels of production should be equal to the workforce available in the economic system under consideration [RONCAGLIA(1978), p.26].

Let us rewrite system (5.10) in the following form:

$$p_1 q_1 = L_1 + (A_{11}p_1 + A_{21}p_2)(1+r)$$

$$p_2 q_2 = L_2 + (A_{12}p_1 + A_{22}p_2)(1+r) \tag{5.11}$$

where q_j, L_j, A_{ij} are gross output, primary inputs and produced inputs in industry $j(=1,2)$, respectively. For sake of simplicity we assume that both commodities are basics.

Differentiating (5.11) with respect to time (holding constant r) we obtain:

$$\dot{p}_1 q_1 + p_1 \dot{q}_1 = \dot{L}_1 + \rho \left(A_{11}\dot{p}_1 + \dot{A}_{11}p_1 + A_{21}\dot{p}_2 + \dot{A}_{21}p_2 \right)$$

$$\dot{p}_2 q_2 + p_2 \dot{q}_2 = \dot{L}_2 + \rho \left(A_{12}\dot{p}_1 + \dot{A}_{12}p_1 + A_{22}\dot{p}_2 + \dot{A}_{22}p_2 \right) \tag{5.12}$$

where $\rho = (1+r)$ and the dot denotes the first derivative respect to time.

Dividing both sides of (5.12) by $p_j q_j$ $(j=1,2)$, we obtain

$$\frac{\dot{p}_1 q_1 + p_1 \dot{q}_1}{p_1 q_1} = \frac{\dot{L}_1}{p_1 q_1} + \rho \left[\left(\frac{A_{11}\dot{p}_1 + A_{21}\dot{p}_2}{p_1 q_1} \right) + \left(\frac{\dot{A}_{11}p_1 + \dot{A}_{21}p_2}{p_1 q_1} \right) \right]$$

$$\frac{\dot{p}_2 q_2 + p_2 \dot{q}_2}{p_2 q_2} = \frac{\dot{L}_2}{p_2 q_2} + \rho \left[\left(\frac{A_{12}\dot{p}_1 + A_{22}\dot{p}_2}{p_2 q_2} \right) + \left(\frac{\dot{A}_{12}p_1 + \dot{A}_{22}p_2}{p_2 q_2} \right) \right] \tag{5.13}$$

We can rewrite system (5.13) for the rates of growth of q_j, L_j and p_i.

$$\hat{p}_1 + \hat{q}_1 = v_{o1}\hat{L}_1 + v_{11}\hat{p}_1 + v_{21}\hat{p}_2 + v_{11}\hat{A}_{11} + v_{21}\hat{A}_{21}$$

$$\hat{p}_2 + \hat{q}_2 = v_{o2}\hat{L}_2 + v_{12}\hat{p}_1 + v_{22}\hat{p}_2 + v_{12}\hat{A}_{12} + v_{22}\hat{A}_{22} \tag{5.14}$$

where the coefficients v_{ij} are the *input value shares* in industry j and are defined as

$$v_{ij} = \frac{L_j}{p_j q_j}, \quad i = 0 \quad \text{(share of wages in gross output)}$$

$$v_{ij} = \rho \frac{p_i A_{ij}}{p_j q_j}, \quad i = 1, 2 \quad \text{(share of gross profits on input}$$

$$1 \text{ and } 2 \text{ in gross output)}$$

therefore $\displaystyle\sum_{i=0}^{2} v_{ij} = 1 \quad \forall j$.

It is now time to consider the effects of the division of labour, i.e. the presence of dynamic increasing returns. To do so we introduce the following 'progress relation':

$$\hat{A}_{ij} - \hat{q}_j = -c_{ij} - d_{ij}\hat{q}_j \qquad [i = 0,1,2 \ ; \quad j = 1,2] \qquad (5.15)$$

namely

$$\hat{A}_{ij} = -c_{ij} + (1 - d_{ij})\,\hat{q}_j$$

where $\hat{A}_{oj} = \hat{L}_j$ and c_{ij}, d_{ij} are constant ($c_{ij} \geq 0$, $0 \leq d_{ij} \leq 1$). According to this expression, inputs per unit of product are negatively related to increases in output as an effect of the organizational and technical changes connected with the division of labour.[15] Obviously, as far as the labour input is concerned, expression (5.15) is equivalent to the progress function. Substituting expression (5.15) for A_{ij} in the system (5.14) we obtain

$$\hat{q}_1 = v_{o1}[-c_{o1} + (1 - d_{o1})\hat{q}_1] + v_{11}[-c_{11} + (1 - d_{11})\hat{q}_1] +$$
$$+ v_{21}[-c_{21} + (1 - d_{21})\hat{q}_1] + (v_{11} - 1)\hat{p}_1 + v_{21}\hat{p}_2$$

$$(5.16)$$

$$\hat{q}_2 = v_{o2}[-c_{o2} + (1 - d_{o2})\hat{q}_2] + v_{12}[-c_{12} + (1 - d_{12})\hat{q}_2] +$$
$$+ v_{22}[-c_{22} + (1 - d_{22})\hat{q}_2] + v_{12}\hat{p}_1 + (v_{22} - 1)\hat{p}_2$$

---

[15]Labour input is commonly saved in the course of scale increases by readjustments in tasks which also entail changes in the composition of man-hour inputs. The level of purchased inputs can be reduced not only by reducing the amount of wasted materials but also by shifting from some kind of materials to others, and by altering qualitative specifications to fit more exactly the planned adjustments in output. Cf. Babbage's considerations about the advantages of the division of labour (both physical and mental) in §2.2.2 .

Solving for p_i we have

$$(1 - v_{11})\hat{p}_1 - v_{21}\hat{p}_2 \;=\; -\sum_{i=0}^{2} v_{i1} c_{i1} - \sum_{i=0}^{2} v_{i1} d_{i1} \hat{q}_1$$

$$\text{(5.17)}$$

$$-v_{12}\hat{p}_1 + (1 - v_{22})\hat{p}_2 \;=\; -\sum_{i=0}^{2} v_{i2} c_{i2} - \sum_{i=0}^{2} v_{i2} d_{i2} \hat{q}_2$$

Let us define $c_j = \sum_{i=0}^{2} v_{ij} c_{ij}$ a weighted average of the c_{ij} (for $j = 1, 2$)
and analogously $d_j = \sum_{i=0}^{2} v_{ij} d_{ij}$ a weighted average of the d_{ij}. System (5.17) becomes

$$(1 - v_{11})\hat{p}_1 - v_{21}\hat{p}_2 \;=\; -c_1 - d_1 \hat{q}_1$$

$$\text{(5.18)}$$

$$-v_{12}\hat{p}_1 + (1 - v_{22})\hat{p}_2 \;=\; -c_2 - d_2 \hat{q}_2$$

and in matrix form

$$\hat{p} = -(c_1 + d_1 \hat{q}_1 \;,\; c_2 + d_2 \hat{q}_2)(I - V)^{-1} \qquad \text{(5.19)}$$

where $V = \begin{pmatrix} v_{11} & v_{12} \\ v_{21} & v_{22} \end{pmatrix}$ is the non-singular matrix of the shares of gross profits on produced inputs and $\hat{p} = (\hat{p}_1, \hat{p}_2)$ is the row vector of the rates of growth of the labour-commanded prices.

The same result can be extended to the case of an n–commodity economy. Expression (5.18) becomes

$$(1 - v_{jj})\hat{p}_j - \sum_{i \neq j} v_{ij} \hat{p}_i \;=\; -c_j - d_j \hat{q}_j$$

and in matrix form

$$\hat{p} = -(c_1 + d_1 \hat{q}_1, \cdots, c_n + d_n \hat{q}_n)(I - V)^{-1} \qquad \text{(5.20)}$$

where V is now a $n \times n$ non-singular matrix.

We must now embark on a careful examination of the economic meaning and implications of expressions (5.19) and (5.20). In both expressions, variations in prices are described as a function of three economic factors: 1) variations in gross outputs, due to increasing division of labour and technical change (as expressed by the progress function); 2) exogenous technical change (represented by the constant c_j); 3) input value shares, which we may consider as *data*, at a given instant of time.[16]

This result reflects the different sets of effects which variations of the technical coefficients bring into being. On the one side (let us say, on the production side) technical change means a variation in the methods of production and, therefore, a change in the physical quantities of goods which may be produced out of a given set of physical inputs. On the other side (let us say, on the demand side), it means a change in the amount of per capita real income at the disposal of consumers in general, and therefore a change in their potential demand. For the sake of simplicity, we prefer to distinguish between these two effects: in this context, we consider the input value shares as a datum in order to isolate *in vacuum* the 'production effects' represented by the feedback relationship linking productivity growth and output growth.

Let us now add a few more considerations about expression (5.19), under the assumption of given v_{ij}. Inverting the system matrix we obtain

$$\hat{p}_1 = -(c_1 + d_1\hat{q}_1)\left[\frac{(1 - v_{22})}{det(I - V)}\right] - (c_2 + d_2\hat{q}_2)\left[\frac{v_{21}}{det(I - V)}\right]$$

$$(5.21)$$

$$\hat{p}_2 = -(c_1 + d_1\hat{q}_1)\left[\frac{v_{12}}{det(I - V)}\right] - (c_2 + d_2\hat{q}_2)\left[\frac{1 - v_{11}}{det(I - V)}\right]$$

---

[16]It is important to remember that, in economics, there are — rigorously speaking — no constants, since all magnitudes one may be dealing with, are, in fact, variable. This is why it sounds more appropriate to speak about *data* (i.e., magnitudes which have to be accepted as given), and *unknowns* (i.e., magnitudes which have to be explained); or, alternatively, to specify the distinction between variables and constants in terms of long-run trends in time, quite irrespective of whether the magnitudes concerned represent unknowns or data [cf. PASINETTI(1981), pp.79-80].

To define the sign of the relationship between variations in quantities and variations in prices we have to find out whether the $det(I-V)$ is positive or negative. It is easy to show that it is indeed positive. Recalling that $\sum_{i=0}^{2} v_{ij} = 1$ $\forall j$, we have $(1 - v_{11}) = v_{01} + v_{21}$ and $(1 - v_{22}) = v_{02} + v_{12}$. Therefore

$$
\begin{aligned}
det(I - V) &= (1 - v_{11})(1 - v_{22}) - v_{12}v_{21} = \\
&= v_{01}v_{02} + v_{21}v_{02} + v_{01}v_{12}
\end{aligned}
$$

and given that all v_{ij} are, by definition, positive, $det(I-V)$ is positive as well.[17]

This result is compatible with the classical explanation of the feedback relationship linking productivity growth and output growth, *via* reductions in production prices[18]: the increase of productivity is followed by an expansion of the market (i.e. of the potential demand for final output); this, in its turn, increases the division of labour which can promote, through a cost reduction, the growth of production and a subsequent expansion of demand [see Appendix B for a possible treatment of the demand-side relation between $\hat{p}_i$ and $\hat{q}_j$].

Moreover, expressions (5.21) stress that the labour commanded price of a certain commodity decreases as an effect of technical changes not only within its own production process, but also in all industries linked by using the same means of production. As an effect of this 'technological interdependence', relative prices will change through

---

[17]It is important to notice that the conclusions about the sign of $det(I - V)$ are strictly dependent on the fact that v_{01} and v_{02} are not both zero.

[18]*Nota bene:* Solution (5.20) does not allow one to draw any conclusion about money price behaviour, if nominal wages are not considered constant. In fact, $\hat{p}_i = \hat{p}_i^m - \hat{w}$ (where $\hat{p}_i^m$ are market prices and w indicates nominal wages) and according to our model we can only say that when $\hat{q}_j > 0$ the labour commanded price of a certain commodity decreases, i.e. $\hat{p}_i^m < \hat{w}$. However, if $\hat{w} = 0$, we have $\hat{p}_i = \hat{p}_i^m < 0$ and conclusions about money prices behaviour can be drawn. In that direction, attention should also be paid to changes in the qualitative characteristics on inputs (e.g. changes in the proportion of clerical to technical and to higher-level salaried personnel) and to reactions in input markets to resulting changes in demand, also in relation to the prevailing market form. Cf. SYLOS-LABINI(1969), (1986).

time. It can be shown that it is indeed a fluke to observe constant relative prices. According to expression (5.20) we have

$$(\hat{p}_1, \cdots, \hat{p}_n)(I - V) = -(c_1 + d_1\hat{q}_1, \cdots, c_n + d_n\hat{q}_n)$$

i.e., under the assumption of constant relative prices

$$k\,(1, \cdots, 1)(I - V) = (c_1 + d_1\hat{q}_1, \cdots, c_n + d_n\hat{q}_n)$$

for some k. Remembering that, by definition, $v_{0j} = 1 - \sum_{i \neq 0} v_{ij}$ we have

$$k\,(v_{01}, \cdots, v_{0n}) = (c_1 + d_1\hat{q}_1, \cdots, c_n + d_n\hat{q}_n)$$

or alternatively

$$k = \frac{c_i + d_i\hat{q}_i}{v_{0i}} \qquad \forall i \tag{5.22}$$

It is indeed *very* unlikely that condition (5.22) will be satisfied by the $\hat{q}_i$; we can therefore conclude that relative prices will in general vary through time.

The variability of technical conditions and relative prices does actually imply that also the shares of gross profits in gross output are variable. From the definition of v_{ij} we know that, under the assumption of a constant unique profit rate

$$\hat{v}_{ij} = (\hat{p}_i - \hat{p}_j) - (c_{ij} + d_{ij}\hat{q}_j)$$

i.e., the variations of these value shares are the combined effect of relative prices and technology variations. Thus, in the light of our model, the possibility of constant v_{ij}, which Harrod's concept of neutral technical change would require [see KENNEDY(1962)], seems a fluke.[19]

5.4.2   Basics and non-basics

Up to now, we have assumed that each of the commodities is a Sraffa–basic, i.e. enters directly or indirectly into the production of all commodities. We can now introduce non-basic commodities in the system — i.e. 'products which are not used, whether as instruments of

---

[19]On the various concepts of neutral technical change, see STEEDMAN(1985).

production or as articles of subsistence in the production of others'
[SRAFFA(1960), p.7]. Let us start by considering the two commodities case, and suppose that commodity 1 is basic whereas commodity
2 is non-basic. Under these circumstances solution (5.21) becomes

$$\hat{p}_1 = -(c_1 + d_1\hat{q}_1)\left[\frac{(1-v_{22})}{det(I-V)}\right]$$

$$\text{(5.23)}$$

$$\hat{p}_2 = -(c_1 + d_1\hat{q}_1)\left[\frac{v_{12}}{det(I-V)}\right] - (c_2 + d_2\hat{q}_2)\left[\frac{(1-v_{11})}{det(I-V)}\right]$$

given that $v_{21} = \rho\frac{p_2 A_{21}}{p_1 q_1} = 0$, since commodity 2 is not used as an
input in the production of commodity 1 [i.e., $A_{21} = 0$].

Generalizing to the n–commodities case, let the set of basic commodities be composed of commodities $1, 2, \cdots, h$ and the set of non-
basic commodities therefore be composed of commodities $h+1, \cdots, n$.
Denote the matrix $(I-V)^{-1}$ by S, it may now be partitioned as

$$S \equiv \begin{bmatrix} S_1 & S_2 \\ 0 & S_4 \end{bmatrix}$$

where S_1 is a $h \times h$ and S_4 is an $(n-h) \times (n-h)$ matrix (note that
some non-basics may be used as inputs in the production of at least
some non-basics). The sub-matrix S_3 must be zero, for otherwise
at least one of commodities $h+1, \ldots, n$ would be used as a direct
input into at least one of industries $1, \ldots, h$ contrary to hypothesis.

Considering the above partition, solution (5.23) points out an un-
stressed (dynamic) dimension of the distinction between Sraffa-basics
and non-basics. This consists in the different impact that technological changes occurring in other industries — at the level of the individual production process — may have on the labour commanded price
of a certain commodity. According to our model, variations in the cost
of production of a Sraffa-basic depend on all progress parameters —
c_j and dj — and output variations which refer to the production of the
other basics, but are not at all influenced by changes occurring in the
production of non-basics. Viceversa, costs of production of non-basics

are influenced by the process of 'division of labour–technical change' in all basics industries and in any relevant non-basics industries.

This asymmetry between basics and non-basics, has some interesting implications as far as the role played by the various sectors of production in the process of economic growth is concerned. Modifying a famous Kaldor maxim, we might argue that the 'basic sector' of the economy is indeed the 'engine of growth'.[20] The greater the rate of growth of the 'basic sector', the greater will be the effect on the production prices of the produced inputs and the application of the division of labour. The introduction of organizational and technical innovations in the production of basics will increase productivity and the effects of this production improvement will propagate from the basic sector to the rest of the economy, in a cumulative way.

In our view, the importance of this feature of the process of 'division of labour–technical change' is not diminished by the lack of direct empirical applicability. Despite the difficulty of identifying the 'basic sector' in the real economy, our theoretical framework seems more open than others to illustrate some recent features of the process of economic growth, for instance the role played by technical changes which occur in the service sector — many services are nowadays to be considered basics. It may be useful to extend our analysis in this direction.

5.5   Conclusions

In this chapter, we have considered the impact of the process of 'division of labour–technical change' in aggregate terms, by introducing a production model based on the interrelation between industries.

Our analysis has focussed on the self-reinforcing nature of the process of increasing returns generated by the division on labour, the main source of reinforcement being the accumulation of kwoledge, due

----

[20]As is well known, Kaldor's first growth law is summed up in the maxim that the manufacturing sector of the economy is the 'engine of growth':the faster the rate of growth of the manufacturing sector, the faster will be the rate of growth of gross domestic product. Our 'law' of growth is, in a certain sense, more exact, given that the set of basic commodities will probably not coincide with the set of manufactured goods.

to improvements by practice. For this reason, we have revised the concept of a progress function (i.e. labour input per unit of product declines as cumulative output increases) in the light of the conclusions drawn in the previous chapter about the long-period behaviour of the stochastic process of intra-firm division of labour. The substantial difference between our concept of a progress function and the traditional engineering one is that the latter refers to the utilization of a given technique whereas ours considers the flow of innovations (technological, organizational etc.) to which the division of labour gives rise. In particular, the coefficient of the progress function (the so-called 'progress elasticity') may be interpreted as an 'average innovation ratio' and such a view paves the way to identifying the factors which influence the response of productivity growth to increase in the output.

Working on the simplest case of Sraffa's model — no fixed capital, no land as a constraint, a single technique and a single product for each industry — and merging it with a 'progress relation' which states that inputs (labour included) per unit of output are negatively related to increases in output, we have made the following points:

- As an effect of the organizational and technical innovations generated by the process of 'division of labour–technical change', variations in production prices are influenced by changes in output which occur in all industries linked by using the same means of production. This also implies that relative prices and input value shares vary through time as an effect of technical change.

- Young's dictum that 'the division of labour depends on the division of labour' is particularly true referring to basic commodities. The introduction of organizational and technical innovations in the production of basics increases productivity and the effects of this production improvement propagate from the 'basic sector' to the rest of the economy, in a cumulative way.

The latter point highlights an unexplored dynamic feature of the distinction between basics and non-basics and, at the same time, provides an interesting insight into the role played by various industries in the process of economic growth.

The former feature is compatible with the classical explanation of the feedback relationship linking productivity growth and output growth, *via* reductions in production prices. It also stresses the existence of a 'ripple-effect': innovations within any industry tend to engender accomodating adjustments in all industries which use the same inputs. In our view, such an effect is not independent of the prevailing market form: for example, in the presence of competition — considered as rivalry in the market place — firms with the lowest cost structure will observe comparative advantages in terms of profits and market shares and this will encourage the introduction of recent innovations in production techniques.

In the light of these considerations, we will turn, in the next chapter, to explore the implications of the division of labour as far as firm behaviour and market forms are concerned.

PART III
IMPLICATIONS FOR THE
THEORY OF THE FIRM
AND MARKET FORMS

PART III

6 Division of labour and theory of the firm

6.1 Introduction

In the first two parts of the book, we have tried to show that the classical conceptualization of technical change, based on the division-of-labour theory, not only considers technical change as an endogenous variable but also allows one, at the same time, to deal with dynamic increasing returns as a factor of economic growth (see Ch.5) and to explore the determinants of the innovative process, at the firm level (see Ch.4).

In this third part we turn to consider the implications of the process of 'division of labour–technical change' as far as market structure and the behaviour of the firm are concerned.

In the following pages, we will first concentrate our attention on the classical concept of competition by trying to identify the role of the division of labour within the competitive process.

It will be stressed that the classical approach analyses competition, not as a state of affairs, but as a dynamic process linking technical change with market behaviour. Competition is defined in the business sense of the word, as a process involving rivalry between producers. Competitive rivalry takes both the form of contests within existing markets, and the form of potential entry into new areas when prospective returns appear relatively attractive. In this it somewhat resembles the modern theory of oligopolistic rivalry and Schumpeter's notion of competition as a process of 'creative destruction'.[1]

This view of competition — which recognizes the link between the process of 'division of labour–technical change' and the evolution of market structure — has strong implications as far as the theory of the firm is concerned. Unlike under perfect competition, firms, in the classical competitive model, are seen as actively seeking the reorganization of production and market activities in the context of rivals' possible reactions.Far from ignoring the business firm, or presenting, as has sometimes been suggested, a pre-industrial view of the economic process, the classical authors noted the importance of the growth of the large, integrated enterprise. 'In those great manufactures' — Smith observed — 'which are destined to supply the great wants of the great body of the people, every different branch of the work employs so great a number of workmen that it is impossible to collect them all into the same workhouse.'[SMITH(1776),p.14]. However, as we will see, the effect of the division of labour in terms of size of the firm may vary according to the nature of the process (or the product) involved and is not predictable 'ex ante'.

6.2   Division of labour and market structure

What we wish to stress in this section is the existence of a link between the process of 'division of labour–technical change' and the evolution of market structure. Division of labour interacts with market struc-

---

[1] For Schumpeter, any realistic analysis of competition would require a shift in analytical focus from the question of how the economy allocates resources efficiently to that of how it creates and destroys them. The entrepreneur is the central figure in the Schumpeterian analytical framework. The entrepreneur plays a disequilibrating role in the market process by interrupting the 'circular flow' of economic life, that is, the ongoing production of existing goods and services under existing technologies and methods of production and organization. He does this by innovating — i.e. by introducing the new product, the new market, the new technology, the new source of raw materials and other factor inputs, the new type of industrial organization, etc. The result is a concept of competition grounded in cost and quality advantages which Schumpeter felt is much more important than the price competition of traditional theory and is the basis of the 'creative destruction' of the capitalist economic process.

ture in at least two ways: 1) it is a weapon of competitive rivalry, in improving the performance of the firm; 2) it leads, in some specific forms, to concentration. In what follows, these two links will be analysed in the light of the classical division-of-labour theory.

6.2.1 The classical concept of competition

In the works of the classical economists competition was identified as a central concept in economic theory. First of all, it was considered inseparable from economic development and was seen as a means of distributing the benefits of technical progress (i.e. of the division of labour in its various forms). Indeed, according to the classical economists,it was the ideal means, from the point of view both of general welfare (the benefits were spread as widely as possible) and of economic development (competition actually promoted further development).

Secondly, the process of competition was considered as an ordering force. In J.S.Mill's words:'Only through the principle of competition has political economy any pretension to the character of a science. So far as rents, profits, wages, prices, are determined by competition, laws may be assigned for them. Assume competition to be their exclusive regulator, and principles of broad generality and scientific precision may be laid down, according to which they will be regulated'[MILL(1848),p.242]. When Smith spoke of competition, it was in connection with the forcing of market price to its 'natural' level. It was not competition and monopoly *per se*, or as market models, which Smith contrasted, but rather the level of prices resulting from the presence or absence of competition as a regulatory force [see McNULTY(1968)].

No writer before Smith presented so effectively the conception of competition as a force which, operating in an atmosphere of 'perfect liberty'[2], would lead self-seeking individuals unconsciously to serve the general welfare. However, he incorporated into the *Wealth of Nations* a concept of competition already well developed in the eco-

---

[2]Smith's conception of 'perfect liberty' consists of the mobility of labour and stock between different uses — the mobility that is necessary for the establishment of 'an ordinary or average rate both of wages and profits'[SMITH(1776), p.72].

nomic literature of his time. That concept was a behavioural one, the essence of which was the effort of the individual seller to undersell, or the individual buyer to outbid, his rivals in the marketplace, and had earlier been employed and developed by a number of writers including Cantillon, Turgot, Hume, Steuart, and others [see McNULTY(1967)].

For Adam Smith, as well as for the other classical economists, competition is characterized by free entry. The tendency toward equality of wage and profit rates in different employments (apart from the inequalities arising from the nature of the employments) presupposes free entry and mobility of labour and stock between different uses.

In the classical perspective, the study of competition proceeds at two distinct levels: analysis of the consequences of given differences between rival firms; and analysis of the procedures and strategies by which firms gain a differential advantage. Indeed, the main concern is with differences generated by various forms of division of labour, that is, 1) differences in the process of production, which relate directly to the firm's knowledge base, the individuals involved and the organizational structure by which their efforts are coordinated (readjustment of production); and 2) differences relating to the ability to innovate, in technological and/or organizational terms, and to create new differential advantages (innovative process).

In production activities, the reorganization of the firm and technical change are seen as the main weapons of competition. Indeed, the intensity of competitive rivalry is related not to the number of firms in the market, but to the number of competitive strategies available to the single firm and to the intensity of the search for competitive advantages through recourse to new production improvements.

The goal of the firm is to capture a transient surplus profit and to transform it into long-run growth potentials, through irreversible technical change and innovation, taking place not in time-continuous form but in discrete steps [see Chs.4 and 5].

The role of profit adjustments is extremely important.[3] In any

---

[3] Indeed, the dynamics of competition can be formalized in terms of deviations of market profit rates from the average 'natural' rate. Once the competitive process is represented as the mobility of capital flows across industries according to differential profit rates (as well as changes in prices due to imbalances in supply and demand) it remains an open question whether the classical natural price and profit rate

market we may expect that firms with the lowest cost structure (in-
herited from the past) will for any given market price have the high-
est profits to finance expansion. In their own pricing policy, firms
are expected to set a price which promises to attract customers and
provides sufficient retained profits to finance the capacity necessary
to serve them. In this way, within markets, relatively low costs will be
associated with relatively fast growth, and a competitive transfer of
market shares from the less to the more efficient will occur. Moreover,
this transfer mechanism may have a feedback effect on efficiency in
the sense that the previously less efficient will be threatened with an
ever-diminishing share of the market unless they can improve their
cost position, for instance by introducing more recent innovations in
production technique.

The transfer and innovation mechanisms within markets thus have
beneficial effects, both upon allocative efficiency, by transferring output and resources to the currently most efficient producers, and upon
technical progressiveness, by encouraging the introduction of the
least-cost techniques available. The outcome of this competitive process, however, in terms of the changing allocation of output between
different firms over time, and the impact of this upon competitive
behaviour itself, will depend ultimately on the answer to a number of
questions about the relationship between past and future efficiency,
and company size and performance [see DOWNIE(1958)].

If past success is repeated, and resulting gains in relative size offer
efficiency advantages in themselves, through economies of scale or
enhanced innovative ability, then particular markets may come to be
dominated by ever fewer, ever larger, firms as a result of the transfer
mechanism, whilst the innovative mechanism, acting as a spur for
past losers to improve performance, may not be powerful enough to
offset this tendency. Past failure may raise the desire, but inhibit
the ability, to recover. Innovation in process (or product) may be
expensive, and low profits, or relatively small scale, may limit the
power of losers to respond actively enough to prevent the transfer
mechanism from leading to the concentration of ever more output in
fewer hands. Thus, in the absence of revival the end product of the

---

system does play the role of a centre of gravity [cf. STEEDMAN(1984)]. See also
ARENA(1978).

competitive process may be domination of the market by the single producer whose efficiency in the past has outstripped all rivals or, less dramatically, by a small number of producers who have gathered economic advantages.

6.2.2   Concentration

The emphasis on the advantages of the firm's internal efficiency led classical authors to a great tolerance for large-sized business organizations.[4]

As we recalled in Ch.2, both Babbage and J.S.Mill connected the intra-firm division of labour and the process of concentration, characterized by non-negligible technological discontinuities. According to the *principle of numerical proportions*, only large firms can apply certain methods, both technical and organizational, and only large firms can realize certain economies of 'size'.[5] And the transition from small to large firms is not gradual; there are jumps and the jumps become broader as concentration proceeds.

Let us recall an observation made by Adam Smith in Chapter 8 of the *Wealth of Nations*: 'when the number of entrepreneurs is small, or has become so, they can easily agree among themselves to regulate prices.' This has to be qualified by stating that the process of concentration must be far advanced, because only then can it be assumed that a few large firms are in a position to control a sizeable part of output. The qualification is more significant than the main assertion; it puts us on guard against identifying or confusing the processes of concentration and monopolization. The first does not necessarily imply the second.

Classical economists generally feel that, despite the concentration of capital, monopoly can be avoided due to the fact that any attempt to raise prices artificially would bring new firms into the market. In Babbage's words:

---

[4] It is well known that Smith was very critical of joint stock companies, as he knew them. It is perhaps less known that Smith was in favour of joint stock companies in the case of four activities, whose operations were 'capable of being reduced to what is called routine'[SMITH(1776), Book V, p.756], that is, banking, insurance, canal and acqueduct construction and management.

[5] For the distinction between size and scale see §3.3.

If the supply, or present stock in hand, be entirely in the possession of one person, he will naturally endeavour to put such a price upon it as shall produce by its sale the greatest quantity of money; but he will be guided in this estimate of the price at which he will sell, both by the knowledge that increased price will cause a diminished consumption, and by the desire to realize his profit before a new supply shall reach the market from some other quarter (p.143).

Any monopoly rent is therefore considered temporary in nature due to the dynamic forces of innovation.[6].

This is strikingly in contrast with Stigler's statement that 'either the division of labor is limited by the extent of market, and, characteristically, industries are monopolized; or industries are characteristically competitive, and the [Smithian] theorem is false or of little significance'[STIGLER(1951), p.185].

As is well known, in order to resolve this dilemma Stigler proposes to view the firm as engaging in a series of distinct operations, each exibiting different cost functions — when cost is expressed as a function of the total output of the firm and the cost functions of the various processes are independent. According to Stigler, some functions will have a rising average cost curve, others a U-shaped curve, and others a falling curve. The diagram proposed by Stigler is represented in FIG.6.1.

Y_1, Y_2, Y_3 are three 'functions' of the firm needed to carry out the productive process. The total average cost for the firm is given by

---

[6]As RICHARDSON(1975) stresses, one might argue that the tendency to monopoly will reassert itself in the long run, if not in relation to complete sets of activities, then in relation to the component activities themselves. 'Will we not find, at the end of the road, precisely that state of monopolistic competition described by Chamberlin, the only difference being that differentiation takes place in the vertical as well as the horizontal dimension? One answer to this question, and the most fundamental, is that *the end of the road may never be reached* For just as one set of activities was separable into a number of components, so may each of these in turn become the field for a further division of labour. Any movement to concentration and monopoly, in respect of any one activity, may therefore be set aside in the same way as was the tendency towards monopolization of the set from which it came'(p.357).

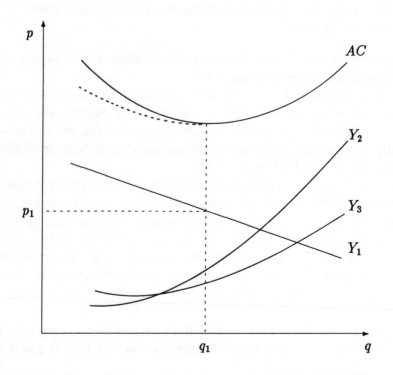

Figure 6.1: **Stigler's diagram**

the vertical sum of all the individual cost functions. According to Stigler's interpretation of Smith's theorem, as the demand for the final product expands it becomes profitable for a firm to allow another firm to specialize in those operations which are subject to increasing returns Y_1 and buy its product (commodity or service) as an intermediate input at a lower price p_1. Referring to the above diagram, as long as the firm produces less than q_1 there is a clear advantage in specializing — measured by the lowering of the total average cost curve AC shown with the broken line (the curve Y_1 is replaced by a horizontal line at a level lower than Y_1 in the effective region). Stigler admitted that the demand for function Y_1 may be too low to justify a new firm specializing in its production. But, with the expansion of the industry, the demand for Y_1 may become sufficient to justify the setting up of a new specialized firm. This firm will initially enjoy a monopoly situation but it will be confronted by elastic demands: it cannot charge a price for the process higher than the average cost of the process to the firms which are abandoning it. With the continued expansion of the industry, the number of firms supplying process Y_1 will increase, so that the new industry may, in turn, abandon parts of process Y_1 to a new set of specialists. On the basis of these considerations, Stigler predicts that vertical disintegration is the typical development of growing industries, while vertical integration will be the typical development in declining industries.

No similar conclusions can be derived from the classical view of the division of labour. Stigler's assumptions are clearly not in the spirit of classical economists who have usually assumed global (dynamic) increasing returns — i.e. average costs decreasing through time — and interdependent productive functions. If we drop the assumption of a U-shaped average cost curve, i.e. a scheme of analysis (coming from Marshall) which has been the object of unanswerable criticisms by SRAFFA(1925), (1926)[7] and, coming much closer to the

---

[7]In these articles Sraffa analyses and criticizes 'the theoretical laws of diminishing and increasing returns, in the form in which they have been used by Marshall as a basis of his theory of value in a regime of competition'. According to Sraffa, classical economists designed the two laws for quite different uses: diminishing returns for the analysis of rent (theory of distribution), increasing returns for division of labour (theory of production). Marshall coordinated this heterogeneous material

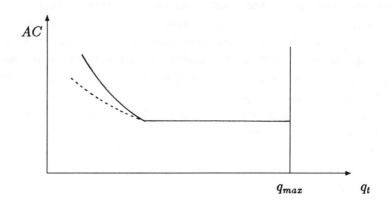

Figure 6.2: **The lowering of the average cost curve**

classical point of view, we consider a decreasing curve [see Ch.3], the
advantage of inter-firm specialization emphasized by Stigler tends to
disappear — there is no substantial lowering of the average cost curve
[see FIG.6.2].

With respect to the inter-dependence of the cost curves, a proper
way of considering the advantages of inter-firm specialization is to
look for the presence of organizational, technical or managerial discontinuities, which may influence the size of the firm. As we stressed
on other occasions, firms tend to introduce organizational innovations
(e.g. better management co-ordination) as an effect of the intra-firm
division of labour. When these innovations are linked to a larger size
of the firm, we will probably observe a tendency to concentration.
Viceversa, if firms find it 'more flexible' to co-ordinate production
by distributing it among small establishments, we will observe the
opposite tendency. Both solutions are compatible with the classical
approach: the predominance of one solution over the other depends

---

in order to obtain a supply schedule (i.e. a functional relationship between costs of
production and quantities of product) to use in his theory of price; 'hence arise its
weak points' [From a letter from P.Sraffa to J.M.Keynes dated 'Milan, June 6,1926';
published in RONCAGLIA(1978), p.11].

on the nature of the process and/or the product involved.[8]

6.3 Division of labour and the role of the firm

With reference to the foregoing discussion, we are now led to ask what are the characteristics given to the capitalist firm by the process of 'division of labour–technical change' in terms of differences in firm behaviour and performance. We first concentrate on the general features of the capitalistic firm and then we turn to study the effects of the division of labour in terms of economies of size.

In our view, the assertion that classical economics fails to confront the problem of economic organization, and particularly the role for the firm therein [see, for instance, BLAUG(1958)], appears, indeed, paradoxical, since that is precisely where Adam Smith and most classical authors began. The *Wealth of Nations* opened not with an analysis of how markets organize economic activity but with how production is organized within the firm. It was not the invisible hand of competition in the market but rather the visible hand of cost-conscious and profit-oriented capitalist/managers which was responsible for the organization of work within classical examples of manufactures.

6.3.1 The nature of the firm

As is well known, in standard price theory the firm is considered a primitive atom of the economy, an unindividuated, profit-maximizing agent interacting with similarly unindividuated consumers and factor suppliers in the market economy. Provided that firms maximize, how

---

[8]It seem reasonable to ask why, if firms are competitive and have access to lower unit costs through the expansion of the division of labour, do they not cut their prices prior to the expansion of the market and so expand at the expense of their rivals? The clear answer to this question from within the classical theory of the division of labour is that economies are due, not merely to changes in the size of the firm, but also to structural changes in the firm's production process caused by the inventive activity occasioned by the process of expansion of scale. These improvements through experience take place at random points in time and their outcome is unpredictable *ex ante*. Therefore, the firm cannot cut its price prior to the expansion because it cannot be certain whether it will 'improve' its process of production and thereby lower its costs, in the near future.

they do it is not of great interest or at least importance to economic analysis.[9]

By contrast, within the classical division-of-labour theory, firms are not conceived as powerless economic agents adjusting passively to parametrically given techniques, prices and quantities but as agents actively seeking the reorganization of production and market activities in the context of rivals' possible reactions. Firms are not seen as price takers either but rather as price-setting firms, with their market shares adjusting through the reaction of the rivals, or as quantity-setting firms, with prices and profits determined through market interactions.

Bearing in mind this main distinction, let us try to highlight the characteristics given to the firm by the process of division of labour.

Suppose that, as an effect of the intra-firm differentiation of labour, a number of individuals come together for the purpose of producing a particular commodity: some of them will contribute their skills and labour, others will commit themselves to bring machines to the joint enterprise. We may assume, for simplicity, that they decide to set up production in the form of a single, long assembly line, and that no more than one worker attends each machine.

The team nature of the activities undertaken within the firm creates special organizational conditions. First of all, the process of production needs to be supervised because one agent's productivity influences another's, and because through timing and other details of action a team member may either assist or hinder another's work. Secondly, the need for supervision brings most agents to act under the direction of superiors in a hierarchy. In this context, decisions taken with respect to market opportunities are not dictated only by agents' individual motivations; there are instead rules and directions.

---

[9]By contrast with this view, in recent years, an increasing number of economists have shown interest in the internal nature of firms, in the firm-market relationship, and in related questions: ALCHIAN–DEMSETZ(1972), WILLIAMSON(1975) [taking inspiration from COASE(1937)], JENSEN–MECKLING(1976), NELSON–WINTER(1982) are prime examples. Two broad distinctions feature prominently, in this literature: i)the distinction between frameworks emphasizing the market (or exchange, contractual) character of firms and those emphasizing the hierarchical (or planned) nature of firms; ii) the distinction between analysts viewing organizational form as driven by efficiency considerations and those for whom, on the contrary, it is driven by considerations of control by subsets of agents.

The 'master manufacturer' (we might call him entrepreneur, manager, merchant, etc.) is a key figure in a firm organized according to the principle of division of labour. According to the classical viewpoint, the essence of his contribution is not capital, but organizing ability.[10] The disaggregation of the productive process into tasks of different degrees of skill and complexity enables him to select workers according to their capacity, paying none more than the nature of the task warrants. Moreover, no one else is in such a strategic position to see the needs and opportunities for technological change, since no one else is in a position to look both upstream and downstream, as well as to competitors on either side.

It is to be noted that this role is not necessarily played by the capitalist. The role of strategist tends to fall to managers or, in socialist economies, to technicians and planners. But such a role exists, and someone, according to the process of division of labour, has to be placed high enough to have the wide view that is not available on the shop floor.

The hierarchical nature of the firm responds also to a specific co-ordination problem which arises, despite the complementarity of productive roles, due to the divergent objectives of workers and capitalist. While the textbook theory of the firm typically depicts enterprises as hiring quantities of labour that translate into levels of output by way of a technologically determined production function, at our level of analysis it is more appropriate to say that flows of labour services, which determine output, are a function not only of the type and number of workers employed, but also of internal incentive structures impacting upon motivation of effort and co-operative inclination. It is part of the role of the strategist to study organizational design in terms of solving problems connected both with the co-ordination and optimization of the productive process and with the incentive structure, so as to increase the flow of appropriate labour services per unit of labour payment.

With these qualifications in mind, we may argue that the decision-taking process of 'our' firm cannot be driven only by price signals but, indeed, conforms to efficiency criteria which may be summarized thus:

---

[10]Indeed, also MARSHALL(1920) puts a lot of emphasis on organization, considering it the fourth agent of production [see his p.137].

1) reduction of labour input per unit of production; 2) increase of the flow of appropriate labour services per wage unit; 3) increase of profits coming from a better organization of production.[11]

Firms' decisions aim to improve competitiveness and profitability, without necessarily implying profit maximization. More profit is preferred to less profit; however, no firm has the capacity to enumerate and evaluate all the opportunities open to it: 'rationality' is bounded by the cognitive and intellectual capacities of the organization.

Moreover, the 'past history' of the firm affects the evaluation of current actions in the important sense that behaviours manifested in past situations affect choices among present alternatives. Thus, whereas the firm of textbook microeconomics is a maximizing function distinguished from other firms, if at all, by its cost structure and products, according to a classical viewpoint firms must be distinguished according to their institutional nature. Put differently, each firm, at our level of analysis, must be considered an almost unique institution, which develops — and which likewise can affect changes in — its specific characteristics through learning by experience, over time.[12]

---

[11]To be consistent with the stochastic models of intra-firm division of labour presented in Ch.4, we must add that the efficiency of the firm grows by sudden jerks. Every time an improvement is introduced, productivity jumps up. The growth of a firm's efficiency is thus a stochastic process (continuous in time, discrete in state), in which the development of the state in time will be described by a step function which changes at random points in time . Following STEINDL(1965), we should probably split the single random variable 'efficiency', into two random variables: 1) 'number of improvements' — i.e. frequency of the steps; and 2) 'productivity increase' — i.e. height of the steps.

[12]To be in fashion, we might say that each firm is characterized by a certain 'revealed technological performance'. Underpinning a firm's revealed performance is its knowledge base, that set of human skills and competences, built cumulatively by experience, which define what can be achieved in practical terms. This knowledge exists in the minds of the firm's employees and its application is contingent upon how the organization pools their individual capacities. On the same line of reasoning see the interesting distinction among *efficiency, fitness* and *creativity* of the firm [METCALFE–GIBBONS(1986)].

6.3.2 Division of labour and size of the firm

We can now turn to analyse the effects of the division of labour on the size of the firm. To do this we must distinguish between the gains from inter-firm specialization of production and those from intra-firm differentiation of labour. In fact, whereas the application of this latter kind of division of labour is historically connected with the process of industrial concentration and with market dominance by large firms, the first kind of division of labour may lead to interdependence and co-operation between autonomous and semi-autonomous small or medium sized firms [see RIDOLFI(1985)].

In brief, two questions, at least, call for attention:

1) Why does the differentiation of labour not lead to the appearance of different firms, each one buying the output of the stage preceding and selling to the stage succeeding?

2) Is there any advantage in allowing different firms to specialize in successive stages of production?

To find an answer to the *first question*, let us imagine that a process of production is composed of a certain number of activities and that each activity is carried out by a different firm. In half of these firms (one might imagine), the owner of the machine employs the worker and pays wages, whereas in the other half the worker rents the machine he or she is working with. We may assume that, as an effect of the division of labour, all the inputs are strictly complementary: if one machine is withdrawn from the assembly line, total output falls to zero; if one worker is missing, the consequence is the same.

We must first observe the emergence of conflicting interests over the distribution of the surplus. Since marginal productivities do not supply the criteria for the distribution of product, the division of the surplus becomes a bargaining problem.

Let us consider various forms of coalition, studying how stable and effective they might be.

(i) Consider first how the bargain might go between the machine owner and the worker at one of the work stations, on the presupposition that the total sum going to this work station has somehow been predetermined. Each can threaten the other to withhold input so that their joint income will go to zero. But the bargaining situation is not symmetrical. Despite the fact that both workers and machines might be highly specialized, in comparative terms, there are plenty of workers in the market, but few, if any, substitutes for the specialized machine. This might make us suspect a tendency for the capitalist to walk away with the surplus, leaving the worker with a subsistence wage. But there is also another asymmetry: the worker has many, the specialized machine few, alternative employment opportunities. If, therefore, the worker could threaten to 'fire' the machine, the worker's bargaining position would be very strong indeed.

(ii)   Let us now consider the bargaining situation among the capitalists. Each machine owner can threaten to reduce output and, therefore, everyone else's earnings to zero — until a replacement for the machine can be found. But, again, substitutes for very specialized machines are hard to find. Any agreement about the division of earnings among the machine owners would be extremely unstable. So unstable, in fact, that some organization of production that avoids the complementarities between the highly specialized inputs of cooperating owners might be preferred.

In both cases (i) and (ii), to preserve the advantages of the division of labour some stable organizational form must be found.

A possible solution, of course, is to prevent individual capitalists from owning and controlling specific machines. This may be a good reason for integrating production into one firm. Once a firm is formed, any capitalist who joins has to give up the ownership of his particular machines and accept shares in the firm. The gains from collusion are various.

First of all, it creates a cartel of capitalists that bargains as one unit against workers. This cartel will own all the work stations. It can fire and replace workers; the workers cannot threaten to fire and replace the dedicated machines. In this context, the worker is not going to come out with any part of the surplus (unless, of course, he or she has some firm-specific capital). Unionization will look like labour's best bet in this situation.

Secondly, it permits a better co-ordination of information and knowledge concerning the productive process. As we have stressed above, most advantages related to the division of labour concern a process of learning by experience, over time. Organizational and technical changes involve the use of information drawn from previous experience, which tends to be 'tacit', i.e. difficult to be transferred and diffused. Given the importance of this 'knowledge base' [see NELSON–WINTER(1982)] and the cost of transmitting information among different firms, it appears more effective to integrate the production into one firm than to disseminate it among firms. Of course, these advantages of integration depend on the degree of complementarity among the activities performed by the various firms.

To find an answer to the *second question* — concerning the advantages of the inter-firm specialization of production — we must refer to the characteristics of the activities carried out within the firm and to the nature of the article produced.

In the previous paragraph we have assumed that the activities composing the process of production were strictly complementary (assembly line structure). Indeed, following RICHARDSON(1972) we may distinguish between different cases. Once it is accepted that activities have to be undertaken by organizations with appropriate 'capabilities' (i.e. with appropriate knowledge and experience) we may distinguish between activities which require the same capability (similarity) and activities which have to be matched, qualitatively and/or quantitatively (complementarity). It is elementary that where activities are both similar and complementary they should be co-ordinated within an individual firm. However, when activities are dissimilar their co-ordination may be brought about by different firms either through co-operation (firms agreeing to match their plans ex ante) or by market transactions.

Similar conclusions can be reached referring to the nature of the article produced. The classical authors — especially Marx in his comparison of heterogeneous and serial manufactures — distinguish between products which result from the merely mechanical assembling of partial products made independently (e.g. watches) and those which owe their completed shape to a series of connected processes and manipulations (e.g. pins). In the latter case the internalization of all operations leads to optimizing every single operation and to increasing the total output, together with the size of the firm. Instead, in the first case the same result can be achieved through the externalization of some operation, provided that there is a good level of cooperation between the different firms.

In conclusion, the findings of our analysis show that the effects of the division of labour in terms of firm size are not fully predictable. Many factors may influence the final outcome:

- the emergence of conflicting interests over the distribution of the surplus (bargaining problem);

- the complementarity (or similarity) of the activities performed;

- the nature of the article produced.

According to the combination of these factors, firms will 'choose' their size and the division of labour will lead to the predominance of large or small-medium firms.[13]

6.4 Conclusions

In this chapter we have concentrated our attention on the implications for the theory of the firm of the process of 'division of labour–technical change'.

It has been stressed that the division of labour interacts with market structure in at least two ways: 1) it is a weapon of competitive rivalry, in improving the performance of the firm; 2) it leads, in some specific forms, to concentration.

Unlike under perfect competition, firms in the classical competitive model [mainly characterized by free entry] raise or lower prices, try to change their cost structures relative to their competitors, or do any of the other things done by business firms in an actual dynamic economic system.

The team nature of the activities undertaken within the firm creates special organizational conditions. First of all, the process of production needs to be supervised because one agent's productivity

---

[13]In this context, the economic behaviour of large corporations is better explained in terms of change of the production processes and the organization of the firm and less in terms of a change of market structures [cf. CLIFTON(1977),(1983)].

influences another's, and because through timing and other details of action a team member may either assist or hinder another's work.

Secondly, the hierarchical nature of the firm responds to a specific coordination problem which arises, despite the complementarity of productive roles, due to the divergent objectives of workers and capitalists.

In the presence of division of labour the firm's decision-taking process is driven by efficiency criteria which may be summarized as follows:

- reduction of labour input per unit of production;

- increase of the flow of appropriate labour services per wage unit;

- increase of profits coming from a better organization of production.

The emphasis on the advantages of the firm's internal efficiency leads classical economists to devote attention to large-sized business organizations. However, it would be a mistake to consider monopoly [or oligopoly] as the inevitable outcome of the process of division of labour. As a matter of fact, many factors may influence the size of the firm: 1) the emergence of conflicting interests over the distribution of the surplus; 2) the complementarity (or similarity) of the activities performed; 3) the nature of the article produced; 4) the existence of economies (or diseconomies) of 'size'. The final outcome of the process depends on the combination of these factors and is, therefore, largely unpredictable.

7 Concluding remarks

It is now time to sum up the contributions given by this work. We have dealt, on the one hand, with conceptual problems connected with economists' thinking about technological change and economies of scale and, on the other hand, with methodological problems related to the formalization of these processes of economic change both at micro and macro levels. In both directions we have drawn inspiration from the classical analysis of the nature and the effects of the industrial division of labour and we have concentrated on the process of increasing returns to scale to which the division of labour gives rise.

We have started our 'conceptual' analysis by highlighting the complex nature of the division of labour and its relationship with the process of technical change. Here are some of the findings of our analysis:

- From a micro point of view, division of labour is always at the same time differentiation of labour and ranking of different activities; its results are 1) an increase in the number of workers necessary for the accomplishment of a definite job[1] and

---

[1]All the different kinds of division of labour have something in common: they are all processes in the evolution of an exchange economy in which an economic task is transferred from the one worker hitherto performing it to several workers, the transfer being so made that each of these performs but a separate part of the previous work [see §2.3.1].

2) co-operation [either between workers with different skills or between workers and machinery].

• From a macro viewpoint, the simultaneous increases of labour productivity and number of workers necessary for the accomplishment of a definite job stress the importance of an increase in income, as a necessary condition for the increase of the division of labour.

In this sense the division of labour is limited by the 'extent of the market'[2]: an expansion of the market (i.e. of the potential demand for final output) increases the division of labour which can promote, through a cost reduction, the growth of production and a subsequent expansion of the market.

In calling attention to the contributions of increases in the division of labour as production is expanded, classical authors' penetrating insights encompass not only the re-organization of tasks to take advantage of the benefits of greater specialization in all production activities (i.e. in the progressive subdivision of tasks into simpler, repetitive units), but also three interacting concomitants: changes in the skill composition as well as in the relative volume of labour inputs, changes in the technique of production, and dynamic substitution of machines for workers. In addition, they recognize the associated opportunities, and pressures, to increase the specialization of various other functions — including maintenance, technical improvements efforts and management — and to keep developing better and still more specialized machines as the basis for achieving further gains in efficiency as production is expanded.

We have then concentrated our attention on the economies of scale generated by the intra-firm division of labour: 1) *longer-series* and 2) *parallel-series* scale economies.

The former arise from the fact that, as output grows, opportunities arise for further efficient subdivision of the productive process into a greater number of elementary operations. Moreover, the con-

---

[2] *Nota bene*: The term market is used as in 'making a market' to denote the availability of effective demand, not as an institution — such as a market-place — that facilitates the process of exchange.

sequent simplification of tasks may allow machines to perform them, and mechanization, in turn renews the sources of economies of scale.

The latter concern the fact that the division of labour can double the output simply by doubling the utilization rate of an idle worker and/or machine, creating new parallel lines of production, nested together.[3]

In brief, both these kinds of internal economies of scale manifest themselves by an increase in the number of operations which compose the process of production, either in the form of new stages of production or as replications of operations already performed.

In both cases the process of 'division of labour–technical change' presents two essential features:

- the ordering — it proceeds by a succession of steps (subsequent increases in the number of operations performed within the productive process), each of which represents a certain increase of productivity due to organizational and/or technical innovation;

- the element of time — which elapses between one step and the following one and which must be regarded as a random variable, because of the unpredictability of changes.

Moreover, the process of increasing returns to scale so generated is inherently knowledge-driven and, therefore, irreversible. Extensions of scale imply the need of searching for additional technological knowledge by considering the possibilities of modifying past practices and evaluating their prospective effects. These may involve altering material specifications, equipment characteristics, input proportions, operating speeds and conditions, labour tasks, maintenance requirements etc..

All these processes are not unidirectional. Improvements in technology also tend to alter the potentials of specialization and, hence, the prospective benefits of further increases in scale. Moreover such interactions tend to be reasonably continuous because innovations in technology within any subsection of the production process tend to

---

[3] These parallel-series economies are probably never totally exhausted; however, they depend on the division of labour so far as this increases the number of elementary operations to be performed within the productive process [see §3.3].

engender accomodating adjustments in antecedent and subsequent subsections in a kind of ripple-effect — as a result of the unceasing pressure to optimize the effective organization of operations as a whole.

The circular causation between output and technical change is at the basis of the formal representations of the industrial division of labour proposed in the second part of the book .

For the sake of simplicitly, we have carried out our analysis at two separate levels: that of the capacity of firms to generate a particular technological performance ('micro' level); and that of the interaction between firms within a market environment in which their technological differences are resolved into changes of quantities and prices ('macro' level). In the former case we have drawn on stochastic modelling [see Ch.4]; in the latter case we made use of a deterministic model (the progress function), which other economists have previously adopted to describe economic progress [see Ch.5].

The two stochastic models that we have introduced to describe the economies of scale, generated by both subdivision of labour and displacement of labour within a single process of production, have the following characteristics:

- the division of labour is described as a random process of 'selection' between different options, which takes place through time and follows a path which is non-predictable;

- the path that the process takes (i.e. the previous organizational and technical changes) influences the outcome of the process of selection, increasing (or reducing) the probabilities of occurrence of the alternative events;

- the long-run behaviour of the process of division of labour shows the emergence of regularity (in the form of a Pareto function), from the 'chaos' of random outcomes. In other words, despite its random nature, the intra-firm division of labour gives rise to a balanced sequence of organizational and technical changes and, in this way, causes a steady increase of productivity.

The microperspective alone does not allow one fully to represent the classical viewpoint. In order to analyse the link between increasing productivity and growth of output, as well as to explore the consequences of the division of labour in terms of behaviour of the firm and different market forms, we must combine the micro analysis with a macroperspective, which considers the economic system as an interrelated whole.

For this reason, in the next step of our analysis we have concentrated on the relation between division of labour and progress functions. In the light of the classical theory, first we have introduced some modifications to the form of the model (as far as the coefficient of the progress function is concerned), apt to emphasize the role of the flow of innovations (organizational, managerial and technical) to which the division of labour gives rise. Secondly, we have 'merged' it with Sraffa's model to consider the industrial operations as an interrelated whole.

The main points of our discussion may be summed up as follows.

- The process of 'learning by experience' which gives rise to a progress function can be described in terms of a probabilistic mechanism, similar to the one illustrated in our stochastic models of intra-firm division of labour.

- The coefficient of the progress function (the so-called 'progress elasticity') may be interpreted as an 'average innovation ratio' and this view paves the way to identifying the factors which influence the response of productivity growth to increases in the scale of production.

- As an effect of the organizational and technical innovations generated by the process of 'division of labour–technical change', production prices are influenced by changes in output which occur in all industries linked by using the same means of production. This also implies that relative prices and input value shares vary through time as an effect of technical change.

- The Smithian theorem that 'the division of labour depends on the extent of the market' is particularly true referring to Sraffa-basic commodities. The introduction of organizational and technical innovations in the production of basics increases productivity and the effects of this production improvement spread from the 'basic sector' to the rest of the economy, in a cumulative way.

Despite the limits of our analysis — due to oversimplified assumptions or to a certain 'naive' approach to advanced mathematical elaborations — we hope to have achieved, in this part of the book, two main goals. On the one side, we have shown the compatibility of the classical conceptualization of technical change with updated, rigorous formal analyses (competing technologies model, progress functions, Sraffa-like models) which aim, as a whole, to constitute an alternative approach to the neoclassical production theory (mainly founded on the production function model). On the other hand, we have indicated a possible way of integrating these different analyses in order to avoid the fragmentation of the analytical contribution, which so often characterizes alternative approaches.

As a result of the steps taken, we have found it useful to analyse technology at two conceptual levels: in terms of artifacts[4], and in terms of the corresponding knowledge bases, the ideas, concepts and modes of enquiry which are necessary to generate a particular production performance. Bridging the two dimensions of technology is the firm, that organization which articulates a knowledge base to design and implement a particular level of performance.

In the last part of the book we have thus turned to study the implications of the process of 'division of labour–technical change' in terms of firm behaviour and its interaction with the market structure.

For this purpose, we have first concentrated our attention on the classical concept of competition by trying to identify the role of the division of labour within the competitive process.

We have stressed that the classical approach analyses competition, not as a state of affairs, but as a dynamic process linking technical change with market behaviour. Competition is defined in the business sense of the word, as a process involving rivalry between producers. Competitive rivalry takes both the form of contests within existing markets, and the form of potential entry into new areas when

---

[4] It should be recalled that throughout the whole book we have not considered product innovations and that major innovations have been considered exogenously determined.

prospective returns appear relatively attractive.

In production activities, the reorganization of the firm and technical change are seen as the main weapons of competition. Indeed, the intensity of competitive rivalry is related not to the number of firms in the market, but to the number of competitive strategies available to the single firm and to the intensity of the search for competitive advantages through recourse to new production improvement.

This view of competition — which recognizes the link between the process of 'division of labour–technical change' and the evolution of market structure — has strong implications as far as the theory of the firm is concerned. Unlike under perfect competition, firms in the classical competitive model raise or lower prices, try to change their cost structures relative to their competitors, or do any of the other things done by business firms in an actual dynamic economic system.

The effects of the division of labour on the size of the firm and hence on its behaviour are not fully predictable. The firm's economic environment is complex and, especially in the presence of division of labour, changes rapidly. There are many factors to be considered: 1)the emergence of conflicting interests over the distribution of the surplus (bargaining problem); 2)the complementarity (or similarity) of the activities performed; 3)the nature of the article produced;4)the existence of economies (or diseconomies) of 'size'. According to the combination of these factors, firms will 'choose' their size and the division of labour will lead to the predominance of large or small-medium firms.[5]

In conclusion, we are well aware that many important analytical steps have still to be taken to develop fully the potentialities of the classical conceptualization of technical change. In our judgment, the main shortcomings of our analysis are perhaps: 1) the insufficient attention dedicated to the effects of the division of labour in

---

[5]It is important to recall that, according to Babbage's principle of numerical proportions, only large firms can apply certain methods, both technical and organizational, and only large firms can realize certain economies of scale.However, despite the concentration of capital, classical economists generally feel that monopoly can be avoided due to the fact that any attempt to raise prices artificially would bring new firms into the market. Any monopoly rent is considered temporary in nature due to the dynamic forces of innovation.

terms of unemployment and changes in the distribution of income[6];
2) our inability to consider explicitly all the determinants of changes
in productivity performance (i.e. potential demand, incentives to investment, comparative behaviour of labour and machinery costs, etc.
— see §3.2); 3) the lack of consideration of the alternative mechanisms
of price determination which may be considered compatible with the
division of labour.

It is in these three directions that we intend to develop our research. In particular, our main interest would be to study the effects
in terms of loss of jobs and price-quantities behaviour of the introduction of constraints to growth (due to technological or organizational
barriers) in both our micro and macro models of increasing returns.
To develop such an analysis would allow us to compare our approach,
on the one hand, with the 'hysteresis' models of unemployment and,
on the other hand, with the game-theory approach to oligopoly. The
main advantage of our analysis — which we derive from the classical
division-of-labour theory — would consist in considering explicitly
the element of time (mainly in terms of 'memory' of the past) and
avoiding any pre-determined outcome (or equilibrium).

---

[6]On this subject, see SYLOS-LABINI(1989).

Appendix A

The aim of this appendix is to provide some explanations of the for-
mulae included in Ch. 4. Although they are mathematical manipulations of secondary importance from an economic point of view, they
are still relevant for understanding how the economic conclusions are
obtained.

Inconsistency of Simon's assumption   It is easy to show that Simon's
assumption, that is:

$$\frac{f(i,m)}{f(i-1,m)} = \frac{f(i,m+1)}{f(i-1,m+1)} \tag{A.1}$$

is inconsistent with the model which has been described.

Let us recall the main equations:

(1) $f(i,m+1) - f(i,m) = \lambda\{(i-1)f(i-1,m) - i\,f(i,m)\}$

(2) $f(1,m+1) - f(1,m) = \alpha - \lambda\,f(1,m)$

(3) $f(i,1) = \delta_{i1} = \begin{cases} 1 & i=1 \\ 0 & i \neq 1 \end{cases}$

(4) $\lambda = \dfrac{1-\alpha}{m}$

(5) $m = \displaystyle\sum_{i=1}^{m} i\,f(i,m)$

We can check the consistency of (A.1) evaluating f(2,3), f(1,3), f(2,2), f(1,2).

From (2) (3) and (4) we obtain

$$f(1,2) - f(1,1) \;=\; \alpha - \lambda f(1,1)$$

i.e.

$$f(1,2) - 1 \;=\; \alpha - (1 - \alpha)$$

namely

$$f(1,2) \;=\; 2\,\alpha$$

From (5) we have

$$2 \;=\; 1\,f(1,2) + 2\,f(2,2)$$

Substituting for $f(1,2)$ we obtain

$$f(2,2) \;=\; 1 - \alpha$$

Analogously from (2) and (4) we have

$$f(1,3) - f(1,2) \;=\; \alpha - \lambda\,f(1,2)$$

and substituting for $f(1,2)$ and λ we obtain

$$f(1,3) \;=\; 2\,\alpha + \alpha^2$$

Eventually from (1) we know that

$$f(2,3) - f(2,2) \;=\; \lambda\,[1\,f(1,2) - 2\,f(2,2)]$$

Substituting for the known probabilities and for λ we obtain

$$f(2,3) \;=\; (1 - \alpha) + (1 - \alpha)\,(2\,\alpha - 1)$$
$$\;=\; (1 - \alpha)2\,\alpha$$

We can now estimate the quotients

$$\frac{f(2,2)}{f(1,2)} = \frac{(1-\alpha)}{2\alpha}$$

and

$$\frac{f(2,3)}{f(1,3)} = \frac{2(1-\alpha)}{2+\alpha}$$

Obviously, they are not equal (except for $3\alpha = 2$ or $\alpha = 1$); therefore Simon's assumption is inconsistent with our model.

Beta and Gamma functions The Beta and Gamma functions to which we refer in Ch. 4 are linked by the following relationship

$$B(p,q) = \frac{\Gamma(p)\,\Gamma(q)}{\Gamma(p+q)} \qquad (A.2)$$

Moreover for a Gamma function defined as

$$\Gamma(\alpha) = \int_0^\infty x^{\alpha-1} e^{-x}\,dx \qquad for \;\; \alpha \;>\; 0$$

the following property is valid

$$\Gamma(\alpha) = (\alpha-1)\,\Gamma(\alpha-1) \qquad (A.3)$$

Applying (A.3) recursively we obtain

$$\Gamma(\rho+i+1) = (\rho+i)(\rho+i-1)\cdots(\rho+2)\Gamma(\rho+2)$$

Therefore according to (A.2) we obtain

$$\frac{(i-1)(i-2)\cdots 3\,2\,1}{(\rho+i)(\rho+i-1)\cdots(\rho+2)} = \frac{\Gamma(i)\,\Gamma(\rho+2)}{\Gamma(\rho+i+1)} =$$

$$= (\rho+1)\frac{\Gamma(i)\,\Gamma(\rho+1)}{\Gamma(\rho+i+1)}$$

$$= (\rho+1)\,B\,(\rho+1,i)$$

Markov processes with absorbing barriers   The model which we have
described in paragraph 4.3.2 does not have absorbing states. In particular, it can be shown that the process does not lock into the zero
state. Let us recall the definition of birth and death rates:

$$\lambda_j = \lambda(1 - \frac{J}{M})\left[\frac{J}{M}(1 - \gamma_1) + (1 - \frac{J}{M})\gamma_2\right]$$

$$\mu_j = \mu(\frac{J}{M})\left[\frac{J}{M}\gamma_1 + (1 - \frac{J}{M})(1 - \gamma_2)\right]$$

where:
M =   constant =   number of elementary operations which may
be either of type A or of type B [A-type = operations performed by
men, B-type = operations performed by machines];
J = $X(t)$ =   number of A-type operations at time t;
γ_1 =   probability that an A-type mutates to a B-type;
γ_2 =   probability that a B-type mutates to an A-type.

It is evident that if $J = 0$ the birth rate is equal to $\lambda\gamma_2$ (i.e.
$\lambda_0 \neq 0$), therefore the zero state is not an absorbing state: the birth
rate is proportional to the probability that a B-type mutates into an
A-type.

It would have been different if we had considered the birth and
death rates as proportional to the number of A-type operations performed at time t — analogously to what we have done in the first
model. In that case we would have had

$$\lambda_j = \lambda J$$

$$\mu_j = \mu J$$

and it is clear that when the 'population' size becomes zero it remains
zero thereafter, i.e. zero is an absorbing state.

Birth and death processes in which the zero state is an absorbing
state arise frequently in stochastic modelling. In these cases it is
of interest to compute the probability of absorption into state zero
starting from state i $(i \geq 1)$. This is not, a priori, a certain event
since conceivably the state variable $X(t)$ may wander forever among
the states $(1, 2, \cdots)$ or possibly drift to infinity.

Let u_i $(i = 1, 2, \cdots)$ denote the probability of absorption into state zero from the initial state i. It can be expressed in terms of the birth and death rates as follows [cf. KARLIN–TAYLOR (1984) p.241-243]:

$$u_i = \frac{\lambda_i}{\mu_i + \lambda_i} u_{i+1} + \frac{\mu_i}{\mu_i + \lambda_i} u_{i-1} \qquad i \geq 1$$

where $u_0 = 1$. Rewriting the above expression we have

$$(u_{i+1} - u_i) = \frac{\mu_i}{\lambda_i} (u_i - u_{i-1}) \qquad i \geq 1$$

Defining $v_i = u_{i+1} - u_i$, we obtain

$$v_i = \frac{\mu_i}{\lambda_i} v_{i-1} \qquad i \geq 1$$

Iteration of the last relation yields the formula

$$v_i = \rho_i v_0 \qquad\qquad\qquad (A.4)$$

where $\rho_0 = 1$ and $\rho_i = \dfrac{\mu_1 \mu_2 \cdots \mu_i}{\lambda_1 \lambda_2 \cdots \lambda_i}$ for $i \geq 1$.

To solve (A.4) subject to the condition $u_0 = 1$ and $0 \leq u_i \leq 1$ we can rewrite it in the form

$$u_{i+1} - u_i = \rho_i (u_1 - 1)$$

Summing these last equations from $i = 1$ to $i = m - 1$ we have

$$u_m - u_1 = (u_1 - 1) \sum_{i=1}^{m-1} \rho_i \qquad m > 1$$

Since u_m is bounded by 1 we can see that if

$$\sum_{i=1}^{\infty} \rho_i = \infty \qquad\qquad\qquad (A.5)$$

then necessarily $u_1 = 1$ and $u_m = 1$ for all $m \geq 2$. In other words, if (A.5) holds then the ultimate absorption into state zero is certain from any initial state.

Applying this criterion to the case of a linear growth birth and death process for which $\mu_j = \mu J$ and $\lambda_j = \lambda J$ $(J = 0, 1, \cdots)$ we obtain $\rho_i = (\mu/\lambda)^i$ and then

$$\sum_{i=m}^{\infty} \rho_i = \sum_{i=m}^{\infty} (\mu/\lambda)^i = \begin{cases} \dfrac{(\mu/\lambda)^m}{1 - (\mu/\lambda)} & when \ \lambda > \mu \\ \infty & when \ \lambda \leq \mu \end{cases}$$

Therefore, the process is sure to vanish eventually only when the individual birth rate λ is less than or equal to the individual death rate. When the birth rate λ exceeds the death rate μ, a linear growth birth and death process can, with strictly positive probability, grow without limit.

There are also some cases in which the growth is bounded. For example, many natural populations exhibit density dependent behaviour wherein the individual birth rates decrease or the individual death rates increase or both changes occur as the population grows. In these cases one introduces the notion of *carrying capacity* (k), an upper bound that the population size cannot exceed, and the population 'fitness' can be measured by the *mean time to extinction* defined as [see KARLIN–TAYLOR (1984)p.245]:

$$w_m = \begin{cases} \infty & if \ \displaystyle\sum_{i=1}^{\infty} \frac{1}{\lambda_i \rho_i} = \infty \\ \displaystyle\sum_{i=1}^{\infty} \frac{1}{\lambda_i \rho_i} + \sum_{k=1}^{m-1} \rho_k \sum_{j=k+1}^{\infty} \frac{1}{\lambda_j \rho_j} & if \ \displaystyle\sum_{i=1}^{\infty} \frac{1}{\lambda_i \rho_i} < \infty \end{cases}$$

Appendix B

A possible demand-side relation   In Ch.5 we have shown how, in the presence of division of labour, variations in production prices are influenced by changes in output. We are aware, of course, that economists usually have in mind also a converse (demand side) relation, running from $\hat{p}_i$ to $\hat{q}_j$. For this reason — although it is *not* our aim to engage in a comprehensive theoretical interpretation of demand — we will now introduce in our model some hypotheses about the evolution of consumers' demand as income increases.

The easiest way of doing this is to assume that the budget shares are constant in value — i.e., expenditure on each good and per capita income grow proportionally. Referring to an Engel curve which plots expenditure for any particular good or service as a function of per capita income, the above assumption implies that the Engel curve is a straight line — whereas, in general, it is more likely to be an S-shaped curve [see FIG.B.1].

To consider consumer demand we must concentrate our attention on the net output of each single industry. Referring to the two commodities case, let us assume, for the sake of simplicity, that the net output of industry j, i.e.

$$n_j = q_j - A_{j1} - A_{j2}$$

is totally consumed. The first step to be taken, to define the converse

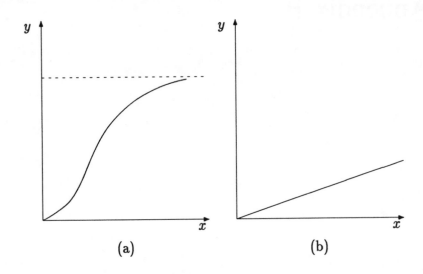

$$x = per\ capita\ income \quad ; \quad y = expenditure$$

Figure B.1: **Engel's curves**

relationship between $\hat{p}_i$ and $\hat{q}_j$, is to express the rate of change of gross output in terms of $\hat{n}_j$.

From the definition of n_j we know that

$$\dot{q}_j = \dot{A}_{j1} + \dot{A}_{j2} + \dot{n}_j$$

i.e.

$$q_j \hat{q}_j = A_{j1} \hat{A}_{j1} + A_{j2} \hat{A}_{j2} + n_j \hat{n}_j$$

Considering the progress relation (5.15) we obtain

$$[q_1 - A_{11}(1 - d_{11})]\hat{q}_1 - A_{12}(1 - d_{12})\hat{q}_2 = -(c_{11}A_{11} + c_{12}A_{12}) + n_1\hat{n}_1 \tag{B.1}$$

$$-A_{21}(1 - d_{21})\hat{q}_1 + [q_2 - A_{22}(1 - d_{22})]\hat{q}_2 = -(c_{21}A_{21} + c_{22}A_{22}) + n_2\hat{n}_2$$

Solving this system for $\hat{q}_j$, we can express $\hat{q}_1$ and $\hat{q}_2$ in terms of $\hat{n}_1$, $\hat{n}_2$. Indicating by M the matrix of the system we have

$$\hat{q}_1 = -\alpha_{o1} + \alpha_{11}\hat{n}_1 + \alpha_{21}\hat{n}_2$$

(B.2)

$$\hat{q}_2 = -\alpha_{02} + \alpha_{12}\hat{n}_1 + \alpha_{22}\hat{n}_2$$

where:

$$\alpha_{01} = \frac{[(c_{11}A_{11} + c_{12}A_{12})(A_{21} + n_2 + d_{22}A_{22})]}{det(M)} +$$

$$+ \frac{[(c_{21}A_{21} + c_{22}A_{22})A_{12}(1 - d_{12})]}{det(M)}$$

$$\alpha_{02} = \frac{[(c_{21}A_{21} + c_{22}A_{22})(A_{12} + n_1 + d_{11}A_{11})]}{det(M)} +$$

$$+ \frac{[(c_{11}A_{11} + c_{12}A_{12})A_{21}(1 - d_{21})]}{det(M)}$$

$$\alpha_{11} = \frac{n_1(A_{21} + n_2 + d_{22}A_{22})}{det(M)} \quad , \quad \alpha_{12} = \frac{n_1 A_{21}(1 - d_{21})}{det(M)}$$

$$\alpha_{21} = \frac{n_2 A_{12}(1 - d_{12})}{det(M)} \quad , \quad \alpha_{22} = \frac{n_2(A_{12} + n_1 + d_{11}A_{11})}{det(M)}$$

We assume $det(M)$ strictly positive, without further discussion here, as only this case gives the appropriate economic meaning to (B.1) — that is, each $\hat{q}_i < 0$ if $\hat{n}_1 = \hat{n}_2 = 0$ and each $\hat{q}_i$ increases with each $\hat{n}_j$.

We have now to connect $\hat{n}_j$ with $\hat{p}_i$. It is with regard to this step that the assumption of constant budget shares is useful. Let us start by considering the total labour input $L = A_{01} + A_{02}$. Differentiating L with respect to time and considering the progress relation we have

$$\dot{L} = A_{o1}[-c_{o1} + (1 - d_{o1})\hat{q}_1] + A_{o2}[-c_{o2} + (1 - d_{o2})\hat{q}_2]$$

Substituting expressions (B.1) for $\hat{q}_1$ and $\hat{q}_2$ we obtain

$$\hat{L} = -\lambda_o + \lambda_1\hat{n}_1 + \lambda_2\hat{n}_2$$

(B.3)

where:

$$\lambda_o = \frac{1}{L}[A_{o1}(c_{o1} + \alpha_1 - d_{o1}\alpha_1) + A_{o2}(c_{o2} + \alpha_2 - d_{o2}\alpha_2)]$$

$$\lambda_1 = \frac{1}{L}[\beta_1 A_{o1}(1 - d_{o1}) + \beta_2 A_{o2}(1 - d_{o2})]$$

$$\lambda_2 = \frac{1}{L}[\gamma_1 A_{o1}(1 - d_{o1}) + \gamma_2 A_{o2}(1 - d_{o2})]$$

Bearing in mind this expression and recalling that, according to the budget shares assumption, $\hat{n}_1 = \hat{p}_2 + \hat{n}_2 - \hat{p}_1$ we obtain

$$\hat{n}_1 = \frac{\hat{L} + \lambda_o - \lambda_2(\hat{p}_1 - \hat{p}_2)}{(\lambda_1 + \lambda_2)}$$

$$\text{(B.4)}$$

$$\hat{n}_2 = \frac{\hat{L} + \lambda_o - \lambda_1(\hat{p}_2 - \hat{p}_1)}{(\lambda_1 + \lambda_2)}$$

Merging expressions (B.1) and (B.3) we can express $\hat{q}_j$ as a function of changes in relative prices, $(\hat{p}_1 - \hat{p}_2)$, and $\hat{L}$:

$$\hat{q}_1 = -\eta_{11} + \eta_{12}\hat{L} - \eta_{13}(\hat{p}_1 - \hat{p}_2)$$

$$\text{(B.5)}$$

$$\hat{q}_2 = -\eta_{21} + \eta_{22}\hat{L} - \eta_{23}(\hat{p}_1 - \hat{p}_2)$$

where:

$$\eta_{11} = \alpha_1 - (\beta_1 + \gamma_1)(\frac{\lambda_o}{\lambda_1 + \lambda_2}) \quad , \quad \eta_{21} = \alpha_2 - (\beta_2 + \gamma_2)(\frac{\lambda_o}{\lambda_1 + \lambda_2})$$

$$\eta_{12} = \frac{(\beta_1 + \gamma_1)}{\lambda_1 + \lambda_2} \quad , \quad \eta_{22} = \frac{(\beta_2 + \gamma_2)}{\lambda_1 + \lambda_2}$$

$$\eta_{13} = \frac{(\beta_1 + \gamma_1)}{\lambda_1 + \lambda_2}(\lambda_2 - \lambda_1) \quad , \quad \eta_{23} = \frac{(\beta_2 + \gamma_2)}{\lambda_1 + \lambda_2}(\lambda_2 - \lambda_1)$$

Appendix B

Working under the assumption of given $\hat{L}$ we can use the above expression to solve the model for $\hat{p}_i$; merging (B.4) with (5.21) we obtain

$$(1 - \gamma_{11})\hat{p}_1 + \gamma_{11}\hat{p}_2 = -\gamma_{o1}$$

$$-\gamma_{12}\hat{p}_1 + (1 + \gamma_{12})\hat{p}_2 = -\gamma_{o2}$$

(B.6)

where:

$$\gamma_{o1} = \frac{1 - v_{22}}{det(I - V)}[c_1 - d_1(\eta_{11} - \eta_{12}\hat{L})] +$$
$$+ \frac{v_{21}}{det(I - V)}[c_2 - d_2(\eta_{21} - \eta_{22}\hat{L})]$$

$$\gamma_{o2} = \frac{v_{12}}{det(I - V)}[c_1 - d_1(\eta_{11} - \eta_{12}\hat{L})] +$$
$$+ \frac{1 - v_{11}}{det(I - V)}[c_2 - d_2(\eta_{21} - \eta_{22}\hat{L})]$$

$$\gamma_{11} = \frac{(1 - v_{22})}{det(I - V)}d_1\eta_{13} + \frac{v_{21}}{det(I - V)}d_2\eta_{23}$$

$$\gamma_{12} = \frac{v_{12}}{det(I - V)}d_1\eta_{13} + \frac{(1 - v_{11})}{det(I - V)}d_2\eta_{23}$$

The above illustration of the demand side of our production model is indeed terribly simple and presents many limitations. In particular, the assumption of given budget shares is very convenient since the income effects are so simple, but, unfortunately, it is not very realistic for the same reason. If there is something that we do positively know about expansion of per capita demand when income increases, this is that per capita expenditure on each commodity does not expand proportionally.[1] All the empirical investigations which have looked into this matter have invariably and without exception found and stressed this result.

---

[1]In general, when income goes up the demand for a good could increase more or less rapidly than income increases. This increase of demand is indeed extremely important for the process of technical change: an increase in productivity, however large it may be, loses much or even all its meaning, if it takes place in the productive process of a commodity for which demand can only be small or negligible.

However, the purpose of our discussion was simply to give an *example* of how to proceed in order to close our model. As we stressed above, we did *not* intend to carry out any serious investigation of demand theory.

Bibliography

ADELMAN,I.G.(1958) 'A Stochastic Analysis of the Size Distribution of Firms', *American Statistical Association Journal*, vol.53, pp.893-904.

ALCHIAN,A.A.–DEMSETZ,H.(1972) 'Production, Information Costs and Economic Organization', *American Economic Review*, vol.62, pp.777-95.

AMENDOLA,M.–GAFFARD,J.L.(1988) *The Innovative Choice*, Basil Blackwell, Oxford.

AMES,E.–ROSENBERG,N.(1965) 'The Progressive Division and Specialization of Industries', *Journal of Development Studies*, vol.1, pp.363-83.

ANDERSON,P.W.–ARROW,K.J.(eds.)(1988) *The Economy as an Evolving Complex System*, Addison-Wesley, New York.

ARENA,R.(1978) 'Note sulla concezione classica della concorrenza', *Economia e Lavoro*, vol. 5, pp.323-52.

ARROW,K.J.(1962) 'The Economic Implications of Learning by Doing', *Review of Economic Studies*, vol.29, pp.155-73.

ARROW,K.J.(1979) 'The Division of Labor in the Economy, the Polity, and the Society', in O'DRISCOLL,G.P.(1979).

ARTHUR,W.B.(1983) *Competing Technologies and Lock-In by Historical Events: the Dynamics of Allocation under Increasing Returns*, IIASA, Paper WP-83-90, Laxenburg; revised as CEPR Paper 43, Stanford, 1985.

ARTHUR,W.B.(1987) 'Self-Reinforcing Mechanisms in Economics', mimeo, Stanford; published in ANDERSON,P.W.-ARROW,K.J. (eds.) (1988).

ARTHUR,W.B.(1988) 'Competing Technologies: an Overview', in DOSI,G. et al.(eds.)(1988).

ASHER,H.(1956) *Cost Quantity Relationships in the Airframe Industry*, RAND Report no.R291.

BABBAGE,C.(1832) *On the Economy of Machinery and Manufactures*, reprint M.Kelley, New York, 1963.

BABBAGE,C.(1851) *The Exposition of 1851*, reprint Gregg International Publisher Ltd., 1969.

BAUMOL,W.J.(1977) 'Say's (at Least) Eight Laws, or What Say and James Mill May Really Have Meant', *Economica*, vol.44, pp.145-61.

BERTING,J. et al.(eds.)(1980) *The Socio-Economic Impact of Microelectronics*, Pergamon Press, Frankfurt.

BLAUG,M.(1958) 'The Classical Economists and the Factory Acts — A Re-examination', *Quarterly Journal of Economics*, vol.72, pp.211-26.

BRAVERMAN,H.(1974) *Labor and Monopoly Capital*, Monthly Review Press, New York.

BÜCHER,K.(1907) *Industrial Evolution*, H.Holt and Co., New York.

CHAMPERNOWNE,D.G.(1953) 'A Model of Income Distribution', *Economic Journal*, vol.63, pp.318-51.

CLARK,J.M.(1923) *Studies in the Economics of Overhead Costs*, University of Chicago Press, Chicago.

CLIFTON,J.A.(1977) 'Competition and the Evolution of the Capitalist Mode of Production', *Cambridge Journal of Economics*, vol.1, pp.137-51.

CLIFTON,J.A.(1983) 'Administered Prices in the context of Capitalist Development', *Contributions to Political Economy*, vol.2, pp.23-38.

COASE,R.H.(1937) 'The Nature of the Firm', *Economica*, vol.4, pp.386-405.

CONWAY,R.W. – SCHULTZ,A.(1959) 'The Manufacturing Progress Function', *Journal of Industrial Engineering*, vol.10, pp.39-54.

CORSI,M.(1983) *La divisione del lavoro nel pensiero degli economisti classici, 1800-1850*, honours thesis, University of Rome.

CORSI,M.(1984) 'Il sistema di fabbrica e la divisione del lavoro: il pensiero di Charles Babbage', *Quaderni di Storia dell'Economia Politica*, n.3, pp.111-23.

CORSI,M.(1986) 'The Classical Conceptualization of Technical Change: Charles Babbage's Contribution', *IIM/LMP-Discussion Papers*, n.8.

COURANT,R. – JOHN,F.(1965) *Introduction to Calculus and Analysis*, vol.I, Wiley and Sons, New York.

DE JONG,J.R.(1957) 'The Effects of Increasing Skill on Cycle Time and its Consequences for Time Standards', *Ergonomics*, vol.1, pp.51-60.

DE JONG,J.R.(1964) 'Increasing Skill and Reduction of Work Time', *Time and Motion Study*, pp.17-28.

DOSI,G.(1984) *Technical Change and Industrial Transformation*, Macmillan, London.

DOSI,G.(1988) 'Sources, Procedures and Microeconomic Effects of Innovation', *Journal of Economic Literature*, vol.26, pp.1120-71.

DOSI,G. et al.(eds.)(1988) *Technical Change and Economic Theory*, Pinter Publishers Ltd., London.

DOWNIE,J.(1958) *The Competitive Process*, Duckworth, London.

EATWELL,J. – MILGATE,M. – NEWMAN,P.(eds.)(1987) *The New Palgrave: A Dictionary of Economics*, 4 voll., Macmillan, London.

ELTIS,W.A.(1975) 'Adam Smith's Theory of Economic Growth', in SKINNER,A.S.–WILSON,T. (eds)(1975).

ELTIS,W.A.(1984) *The Classical Theory of Economic Growth*, Macmillan, London.

FERGUSON,A.(1767) *An Essay on the History of Civil Society*, ed. by D.Forbes, Edinburgh University Press, 1966.

FOLEY,V.(1974) 'The Division of Labour in Plato and Smith', *History of Political Economy*, vol.6, pp.220-42.

FREEMAN,C.(1982) *The Economics of Industrial Innovation*, 2nd. edn., MIT Press, Cambridge(Mass.).

GEORGESCU-ROEGEN,N.(1972) 'Process Analysis and the Neoclassical Theory of Production', *American Journal of Agricultural Economics*, vol.54, pp.279-94.

GEORGESCU-ROEGEN,N.(1976) *Energy and Economic Myths*, Pergamon Press, New York.

GIBRAT,R.(1930) *Les Inégalites Économiques*, Recueil Sirey, Paris.

GIOJA,M.(1815)   *Nuovo prospetto delle scienze economiche,* 6 voll., G.Pirotta, Milano.

GLOVER,J.H.(1965) 'Manufacturing Progress Function I. An Alternative Model and its Comparison with Existing Functions', *International Journal of Production Research,* vol.4, pp.279-300.

GOLD,B.(1981) 'Changing Perspectives in Size, Scale and Returns: An Interpretative Survey', *Journal Of Economic Literature,* vol.19, pp.5-33.

GROENEWEGEN,P.D.(1977) 'Adam Smith and the Division of Labour: A Bicentenary Estimate', *Australian Economic Papers,* vol.16, pp. 161-74.

GROENEWEGEN,P.D.(1987) 'Division of Labour', in EATWELL,J.–MILGATE,M.–NEWMAN,P.(eds.)(1987), vol.1, pp.901-7.

HAMOVY,R.(1968) 'Adam Smith, Adam Ferguson and the Division of Labour', *Economica,* vol.35, pp.249-59.

HART,P.E. – PRAIS,S.J.(1956) 'The Analysis of Business Concentration: a Statistical Approach', *Journal of Royal Statistical Society,* vol.119,pp.150-75.

HICKS,J.(1965) *Capital and Growth,* Oxford University Press, Oxford.

HODGSKIN,T.(1827) *Popular Political Economy,* reprint M.Kelley, New York, 1966.

HORNER,S.M.(1977) *Stochastic Models of Technology Diffusion,* Ph.D dissertation, University of Michigan.

HULL,C.H.(1963) *Economic Writings of Sir William Petty,* reprint M.Kelley, New York.

IJIRI,Y. – SIMON,H.A.(1977) *Skew Distributions and the Sizes of Business Firms,* North Holland, Amsterdam.

JANTSCH,E. – WADDINGTON,C.H.(eds.)(1976) *Evolution and Consciousness*, Addison - Wesley, Reading(Mass.).

JENSEN,M.C.–MECKLING,W.H.(1976) 'Theory of the Firm : Managerial Behaviour, Agency Costs and Ownership Structure', *Journal of Financial Economics*, vol.3, pp.305-60.

KALDOR,N.(1934) 'The Equilibrium of the Firm', *Economic Journal*, vol.44, pp.60-74.

KALDOR,N.(1957) 'A Model of Economic Growth', *Economic Journal*, vol.67, pp.591-624.

KALDOR,N.(1966) *Causes of the Slow Rate of Growth of the United Kingdom*, Cambridge University Press, Cambridge.

KALDOR,N.(1972) 'The Irrelevance of Equilibrium Economics', *Economic Journal*, vol.82, pp.1237-55.

KALDOR,N.(1985) *Economics without Equilibrium*, University College Press, Cardiff.

KALDOR,N.–MIRRLEES,J.A.(1962) 'A New Model of Economic Growth', *Review of Economic Studies*, vol.29, pp.174-92.

KALECKI,M.(1940) 'A Theorem on Technical Progress', *Review of Economic Studies*, vol.8, pp.178-84.

KALECKI,M.(1945) 'On the Gibrat Distribution', *Econometrica*, vol.13,pp.161-70.

KALECKI,M.(1954) *Theory of Economic Dynamics*, Allen and Unwin, London.

KARLIN,S. – TAYLOR,H.M.(1984) *An Introduction to Stochastic Modeling*, Academic Press, London.

KENNEDY,C.(1962) 'The Character of Improvements and of Technical Progress', *Economic Journal*, vol.72, pp.899-911.

KENNEDY,C.– THIRLWALL,A.P.(1972) 'Surveys in Applied Economics: Technical Progress', *Economic Journal*, vol.82, pp.11-63.

KUZNETS,S.S.(1930) *Secular Movements in Production and Prices*, Houghton Mifflin, Boston.

LANDES,D.S.(1969) *The Unbound Prometeus*, Cambridge University Press, Cambridge.

LANDES,D.S.(1986) 'What Do Bosses Really Do?', *Journal of Economic History*, vol.46, pp.585-623.

LANGLOIS,R.N.(1986) *Economics as a Process*, Cambridge University Press, Cambridge.

LEIJONHUFUD,A.(1986) 'Capitalism and the Factory System', in LANGLOIS(1986).

MARCUZZO,M.C.(ed.)(1976) *'Problemi e storia delle teorie economiche'*, Mazzotta, Milano.

MARGLIN,S.A.(1974) 'What Do Bosses Do: the Origins and Function of Hierarchy in Capitalist Production', *Review of Radical Political Economics*, vol.6, pp.60-112.

MARGLIN,S.A.(1984) 'Knowledge and Power', in STEPHEN, F.H. (ed.)(1984).

MARSHALL,A.(1919) *Industry and Trade*, Macmillan, London.

MARSHALL,A.(1920) *Principles of Economics*, VIII ed., Macmillan, London, 1986.

MARX,K.(1867) *Capital*, vol.1, Penguin Books, Harmondsworth, 1982.

McCOMBIE,J.S.L.(1981) 'What Still Remains of Kaldor's Laws?', *Economic Journal*, vol.91, pp.206-16.

McCOMBIE,J.S.L.(1982) 'Economic Growth, Kaldor's Laws and the Static–Dynamic Verdoorn Law Paradox', *Applied Economics*, vol.14, pp.279-94.

McNULTY,P.J.(1967) 'A Note on the History of Perfect Competition', *Journal of Political Economy*, vol.75, pp.395-9.

McNULTY,P.J.(1968) 'Economic Theory and the Meaning of Competition', *Quarterly Journal of Economics*, vol.82, pp.639-56.

McNULTY,P.J.(1975) 'On the Nature and Theory of Economic Organization: the Role of the Firm Reconsidered', *History of Political Economy*, vol.16, pp.233-53.

METCALFE,J.S.– GIBBONS,M.(1986) 'Technological Variety and the Process of Competition', Economie Appliquèe, vol.39, pp.493-520.

MILL,J.S.(1848) *Principles of Political Economy*, Longmans, London, 1909; reprint A.M.Kelley, New York, 1987.

MOMIGLIANO,F. – SINISCALCO,D.(1982) 'The Growth of Service Employment: A Reappraisal',*BNL-Quarterly Review*, n.142, pp.269-306.

NELSON,R.R – WINTER,S.G.(1982) *An Evolutionary Theory of Economic Change*, Harvard University Press, Cambridge (Mass.).

O'DRISCOLL,G.P.(1979) *Adam Smith and Modern Political Economy*, Iowa State University Press.

PASINETTI,L.L.(1981) *Structural Change and Economic Growth*, Cambridge University Press, Cambridge.

PETTY,W.(1671) *Political Arithmetick*, in HULL,C.H.(1963).

PIORE,M.J.– SABEL,C.F.(1984) *The Second Industrial Divide*, Basic Books, New York.

PRESCOTT,R.B.(1922) 'Law of Growth in Forecasting Demand', *Journal of the American Statistical Association*, vol.18, pp. 471-9.

PRIGOGINE,I.(1976) 'Order through Fluctuation: Self-Organization and Social System', in JANTSCH,E. – WADDINGTON, C.H. (eds.) (1976).

RICARDO,D.(1821) *Principles of Political Economy and Taxation*, ed. by P.Sraffa, Cambridge University Press, Cambridge, 1951.

RICHARDSON,G.B.(1972) 'The Organisation of Industry', *Economic Journal*, vol.82, pp.883-96.

RICHARDSON,G.B.(1975) 'Adam Smith on Competition and Increasing Returns', in SKINNER,A.S.–WILSON,T.(1975).

RIDOLFI,M.(1985) *Premessa per una teoria delle imprese minori*, Franco Angeli, Milano.

ROBBINS,L.(1928) 'The Representative Firm', *Economic Journal*, vol.38, pp.387-404.

ROBBINS,L.(1932) *An Essay on the Nature and Significance of Economic Science*, Macmillan, London.

ROMANO,R.M.(1982) 'The Economic Ideas of Charles Babbage', *History of Political Economy*, vol.14, pp. 385-405.

RONCAGLIA,A.(1978) *Sraffa and the Theory of Prices*, J.Wiley and Sons, Chichester.

ROSENBERG,N.(1965) 'Adam Smith on the Division of Labour: Two Views or One?', *Economica*, vol.32, pp.127-139.

ROSENBERG,N.(1976) *Perspectives on Technology*, Cambridge University Press, Cambridge.

ROSENBERG,N.(1982) *Inside the Black Box: Technology and Economics*, Cambridge University Press, Cambridge.

ROWTHORN,R.E.(1975) 'What Remains of Kaldor's Law?', *Economic Journal*, vol.85, pp.10-9.

ROWTHORN,R.E.(1979) 'A Note on Verdoorn's Law', *Economic Journal*, vol.89, pp.131-33.

SAHAL,D.(1975) 'A Reformulation of the Technological Progress Function', *Technological Forecasting and Social Change*, vol.8, pp.75-90.

SAHAL,D.(1980) *Research, Development and Technological Innovation*, D.C.Heath and Co., Lexington (Mass.).

SAHAL,D.(1981) *Patterns of Technological Innovation*, Addison-Wesley, Reading(Mass.).

SCAZZIERI,R.(1981) *Efficienza produttiva e livelli di attività*, Il Mulino, Bologna.

SCHUMPETER,J.A.(1954) *History of Economic Analysis*, Oxford University Press, London.

SHACKLE,G.L.S.(1972) *Epistemics and Economics*, Cambridge University Press, Cambridge.

SIMON,H.A.(1955) 'On a Class of Skew Distribution Functions', in IJIRI,Y.–SIMON,H.A.(eds.)(1977).

SKINNER,A.S.–WILSON,T.(eds.)(1975) *Essays on Adam Smith*, Oxford University Press, Oxford.

SKINNER,A.S.–WILSON,T.(eds.)(1976) *The Market and the State: Essays in Honour of Adam Smith*, Oxford University Press, Oxford.

SMITH,A.(1776) *An Inquiry into the Nature and the Causes of the Wealth of Nations*, ed. by R.H.Campbell and A.S.Skinner, Clarendon Press, Oxford, 1976.

SPANOS,A(1986) *Statistical Foundations of Econometric Modeling*, Cambridge University Press, Cambridge.

SRAFFA,P.(1925) 'Sulle relazioni fra costo e quantità prodotta', *Annali di Economia*, vol.2, pp.277-328; reprinted in *La Rivista Trimestrale*, n.9, pp.177-213, 1964.

SRAFFA,P.(1926) 'The Laws of Returns under Competitive Conditions', *Economic Journal*, vol.36, pp.535-50.

SRAFFA,P.(1930) 'A Criticism' and 'Rejoinder', interventions in 'Symposium on Increasing Returns and the Representative Firm', *Economic Journal*, vol.40, pp.89-93.

SRAFFA,P.(1960) *Production of Commodities by means of Commodities*, Cambridge University Press, Cambridge.

STANBACK,T.M.(ed.)(1981) *Services: the New Economy*, Conservation of Human Resources Series, n.20, Totowa.

STEEDMAN,I.(1967) *The Implications for the Theory of the Firm of the Dependence of Current Production and Market Possibilities on Past Output and Sales*, unpublished Ph.D. thesis, University of Manchester.

STEEDMAN,I.(1970) 'Some Improvement Curve Theory', *The International Journal of Production Research*, vol.8, pp.189-205.

STEEDMAN,I.(1984) 'Natural Prices, Differential Profit Rates and the Classical Competitive Process', *The Manchester School*, vol.52, pp.123-40.

STEEDMAN,I.(1985) 'On the Impossibility of Hicks' Neutral Technical Change', *Economic Journal*, vol.95, pp.746-58.

STEEDMAN,I.(1986) 'Trade Interest versus Class Interest', *Economia Politica*, vol.3, pp.187-206.

STEINDL,J.(1965) *Random Processes and the Growth of Firms*, Griffin, London.

STEINDL,J.(1974) *Technical Progress, Distribution and Growth*, mimeo, Vienna.

STEINDL,J.(1980) 'Technical Progress and Evolution', in SAHAL(1980).

STEPHEN,F.H.(ed.)(1984) *Firms, Organization and Labour*, Macmillan, London.

STIGLER,G.(1951) 'The Division of Labour Is Limited by the Extent of the Market', *Journal of Political Economy*, vol.59, pp.185-93.

STONEMAN,P.(1983) *The Economic Analysis of Technological Change*, Oxford University Press, Oxford.

SYLOS-LABINI,P.(1969) *Oligopoly and Technical Progress*, II ed. revised, Harvard University Press, Cambridge(Mass.).

SYLOS-LABINI,P.(1982) *Lezioni di economia - Microeconomia*, Ateneo, Roma.

SYLOS-LABINI,P.(1984) *The Forces of Economic Growth and Decline*, MIT Press, Cambridge (Mass.).

SYLOS-LABINI,P.(1986) 'Oligopolio e progresso tecnico: una riconsiderazione critica dopo trent'anni', *L'Industria*, vol.7, pp.587-603.

SYLOS-LABINI,P.(1989) *Nuove tecnologie e disoccupazione*, Laterza, Bari.

TALAMO,A.(1976) 'Piero Sraffa: su alcuni problemi di interpretazione', in MARCUZZO(1976), pp.45-93.

THIRLWALL,A.P.(1980) 'Rowthorn's Interpretation of Verdoorn's Law', *Economic Journal*, vol.90, pp.386-8.

VERDOORN,P.J.(1949) 'Fattori che regolano lo sviluppo e la produttività del lavoro', *L'Industria*, vol.1, pp.45-53.

VERDOORN,P.J.(1956) 'Complementarity and Long-Range Projections', *Econometrica*, vol.24, pp.429-50.

VERDOORN,P.J.(1980) 'Verdoorn's Law in Retrospect: A Comment', *Economic Journal*, vol.90, pp.382-5.

WEITZMAN,M.L.(1983) 'Some Macroeconomic Implications of Alternative Compensation Systems', *Economic Journal*, vol.93, pp.763-83.

WEST,E.G.(1964) 'Adam Smith's Two Views on the Division of Labour', *Economica*, vol.31, pp.23-32.

WILLIAMS,P.L.(1978) *The Emergence of the Theory of the Firm: from A.Smith to Alfred Marshall*, Macmillan, London,1978.

WILLIAMSON,O.E.(1975) *Market and Hierarchies*, Free Press, New York.

WOLFE,J.N.(1968) 'Productivity and Growth in Manufacturing Industry: Some Reflections on Professor Kaldor's Inaugural Lecture', *Economica*, vol.35, pp.116-26.

WRIGHT,T.P.(1936) 'Factors affecting the Cost of Airframes', *Journal of the Aeronautical Sciences*, vol.3, pp.122-8.

YOUNG,A.(1928) 'Increasing Returns and Economic Progress', *Economic Journal*, vol.38, pp.527-42.

ZIPF,G.K.(1949) *Human Behaviour and the Principle of Least Effort*, Addison-Wesley, Cambridge(Mass.).